Accident Patterns

Priscilla M. Gilbert

Previously published in two volumes, which have been combined in the current printing.

Copyright 2012
All rights reserved.

No part of this book may be reproduced or transcribed in any form or by any means, electronic or mechanical, including photocopying or recording or by any information storage and retrieval system without written permission from the author and publisher, except in the case of brief quotations embodied in critical reviews and articles. Requests and inquiries may be mailed to: American Federation of Astrologers, Inc., 6535 S. Rural Road, Tempe, AZ 85283.

ISBN-10: 0-86690-634-7
ISBN-13: 978-0-86690-634-0

Cover Design: Jack Cipolla

Published by:
American Federation of Astrologers, Inc.
6535 S. Rural Road
Tempe, AZ 85283

www.astrologers.com

Printed in the United States of America

Contents

Introduction   v

Part I: Fatal Accidents

Plane Crash	3
Hit by Car	9
Hit by Train	17
Head-on Car Collision	31
Hit by Car	39
Skid into Telephone Pole	47
Car Crash into Embankment	55
Car Collision	61
Accidental Electrocution	69
Hit by Truck	77
Death by Fall	85

Part II: What Saved Them

Drove into Drainage Ditch	97
Truck Rollover	105
Head-on Collision	113
Fall from Motorcycle	121
Fell Off Cliff	129

Hit by Train	137
Shattered Foot	143
Train Crash	149
Third-degree Burns	155
Motorcycle Accident	163
Car Accident	169
Car Crash	173
Car Accident	183

Introduction

To everything there is a season, and a time to every purpose under the heaven: A time to be born, and a time to die; a time to plant, and a time to pluck up that which is planted.—Ecclesiastes 3:1.

Some call it fate. Some call it destiny. I call it potential.

An accident, so-labeled, means a happening that is not intended or expected; yet in this cosmos of law and order, there really is no such thing as an accidental event. Unexpected to our mind and to our mundane consciousness—yes! But accidental? No!

I find, however, that regardless of the fact that we all follow the tendencies and potentials as indicated in our individual charts 99.9 percent of the time, there is still that x-factor, the one percent factor that is the human's freedom, not of will, but of choice. It certainly involves the exercise of the will of the individual, wherein if the tendency or potential cannot be completely changed, it sometimes at least can be altered or mitigated to a lesser or greater degree.

To be forewarned is to be forearmed, and this to me is one of the best reasons for each individual to know the potential pattern of his or her natal chart, which I call the roadmap of life's journey.

For example, there was a major plane crash in New York City in 1975. All the persons involved needed the experience of the event, but for some of them it was not the chosen time of their passing over, so they survived the crash. Then there have been cases where a person received a strong impression or feeling, and backed away from taking a certain plane which later crashed; that person had no need of that experience at that time.

I believe that before the birth of the entity the incoming soul, the true God-man, exercising God-given free will, picks a certain pattern to work on in the coming life. Then, when the stars' positions reflect that chosen pattern, the individual is born into the earth plane of manifestation, and the chart then becomes his or her roadmap for the journey through this life. This map shows the potential for pressures coming from within and from without.

In this crowded world there is always some sort of involvement with others, and there are many outside circumstances, which in astrology are called transits and over which we have little or no control. Thus to me the stars neither impel nor compel; they only reflect the pressures the individual is undergoing. Sometimes it is hard for an individual to control his or her inner pressures, so how much less is the individual able to control outside events?

Since there is a season for all things, then there must be a cosmic clock, a life rhythm to which we individually respond, and this—the potential for events—is reflected or shown on the life map of the chart.

The natal chart can be compared to the face of a clock, wherein is contained the entire potential of character tendencies and probable events. Twelve numbers on the face of the clock and twelve houses, or departments of life, in the chart.

Although the potential is there at the moment of birth, it is not all expressed at that moment. As the large hand of the clock ticks off the minutes, so in a chart the progressions bring certain potential developments into focus.

Then the smaller hand on the clock says it is two o'clock, or five o'clock, or ten, and so the progressed Moon, the timer of events, says this is the approximate month. Then the transiting planets (where they are today), representing outside circumstances, and the aspects they make to a chart say this is the day for an event, whether it is to begin a new study, to get married, to have a child, to make a move, or to step on a nail.

Thus does the cosmic rhythm establish the timing of all things. To be forewarned is to be forearmed, and this to me is one of the best reasons for each individual to know the potential pattern of his or her natal chart, which I call the road map of life's journey.

As an example, there was a major plane crash in New York City in 1975. All of the people involved needed the experience of the event, but for some it was not the chosen time of their passing over, so they survived the crash. There have been cases where a person received a strong impression or feeling and backed away from taking a certain plane that later crashed. That person had no need of that experience at that time.

I believe that before the birth of the entity, the incoming soul picks a certain pattern to work on in the coming life. Then, when the stars' positions reflect that chosen pattern, the individual is born into the Earth plane of manifestation, and the chart then becomes the road map for the journey through this life. This map shows the potentiality of pressures coming from within and from without.

In this crowded world there is always some sort of an involvement with others, and there are many outside circumstances over which we have little or no control. Thus, to me, the stars neither impel nor compel; they only reflect the pressures that the individual is undergoing. Thus does the cosmic rhythm establish the timing of all things.

Even as a beginning student of astrology I was very interested in finding the potential for accidents as shown in the natal horoscope. As I tell my students, it is a direct interest, stemming from the fact that I belong to an accident-prone family. This is what has led me to do much study and research on this subject.

When looking for accident patterns in the natal chart, I first note whether there are planets in the violent signs of Aries, Scorpio, or Capricorn. The next thing I note are planets or cusps at critical degrees, which are zero, thirteen, and twenty-six of the cardinal signs, nine and twenty-one of the fixed signs, and four and seventeen of the mutable signs. Planets conjunct fixed stars can also be indicative of such a potential, and so can planets at the same degree as the lunar nodes.

For travel accidents, the third and ninth houses are of prime importance; they rule short trips (third) and long journeys (ninth).

Any malefic (so-called because we usually do not like the results of the activity they represent) posited in either or both of these houses, as well as their aspects, especially to the lights (Sun and Moon), are other factors to be taken into consideration.

Malefics elevated above the lights can also indicate a potential for a violent end to the life, while any planet in the fourth and ninth houses, as well as their rulers and the ruler of the Ascendant, are important. Planets and cusps at the twenty-ninth degree of any sign also carry a warning as they are constantly "running out of rope," unable to function properly. The more involvement there is in a chart of the different types of danger signals, the greater the potential that the individual will be accident prone.

The kind of injury is usually described by the planets which are involved. Thus:

- Mars rules cuts, burns, firearms, and concussions.
- Saturn rules fractures and falls, as well as blows from blunt instruments; thus it would be involved in plane disasters because of the fall.
- Uranus rules electricity, explosions, and any sudden and unexpected events.
- Neptune rules drugs, gases, coma, and drowning.
- Pluto rules rape and kidnaping; it crushes and suffocates.

- Mercury rules cars and motorcycles.
- While Jupiter is not labeled as a malefic and is known as the greater benefic, it can at times, by its very nature, cause excessive bleeding and thus hemorrhages.

Any of the foregoing posited in violent signs increases the potential for accidental events.

The midpoint of Mars and Uranus is always the accident-prone point of any chart, while the midpoint of Mars and Saturn is always the point of greatest danger in any chart.

If the birth time given is accurate, then the Arabic Parts of (D) Death, (F) Fatality, or (C) Catastrophe, and (P) Peril, will always register at the time of such an event.

It takes a lot to end a life as we tend to cling to it, so the progressions in force will be very strong, and there will always be more than one aspect pointing out the probable event. I have found that the planets making the aspects in the transits will be the same ones active in the progressions. I also use primary and tertiary directions as confirmation of a potential accident.

In cases of violent death there is usually an interplay of almost all of the radix, progressed, tertiary, and transiting planets.

The widest orb used in the transiting aspects is four to six degrees. The ruler of one travel house in the other travel house is also indicative of a potential accident. In using the eclipses preceding the event I did not here consider the other transiting planets, but they are also very important as indicators of oncoming activity.

In Part II, we look at accident potentials such as are covered in Part I, with the big difference that the people survived their experience. What saved them?

There is less potential for violence in these charts as compared to those in Part I.

Jupiter, the greater benefic, and/or Venus, the lesser benefic, is in good aspect, such as a trine, to the Ascendant, Sun, Moon, or Mercury.

Unless another vehicle is involved in the event, there will not be as much emphasis on the third and ninth house placements and afflictions.

There is also less pressure from the fixed stars, and less total involvement of the natal, progressed, and transiting planets.

Formulas for Arabic Parts

- (D) Death = Ascendant + Eighth Cusp - Moon
- (F) Fatality = Ascendant + Saturn - Sun
- (C) Catastrophe = Ascendant + Uranus - Saturn
- (P) Peril = Ascendant + Ruler of Eighth - Saturn
- (S) Surgery = Ascendant + Saturn - Mars
- (PC) Plane Crash = Ascendant + Ninth Cusp - Pluto (I discovered this one during my research.)

Tertiary directions can be calculated in most astrological software programs.

Part I
Potential Fulfilled:
Fatal Accidents

Chapter 1

Plane Crash

This woman died while in pursuit of her career; she and her co-workers were killed instantly when their chartered plane crashed on March 13, 1974, at approximately 4:30 pm.

In this chart, Ascendant-ruler Mars is in the violent sign Aries. Mars is co-ruler of the eighth house and conjunct Saturn in the public seventh, with both planets in violent Scorpio.

Sun, Venus, and Mercury are also in a violent sign, with Mercury ruling the third house of travel. All three are in the tenth house of career, with Venus and Mercury forming a conjunction. Thus, she will seek a career that puts her in the public eye.

Jupiter, ruler of the ninth house, is in the third, while the Sagittarius Moon is in the ninth; the two planets are in T-square with the Part of Fortune, which, in the twelfth, and in Pisces, becomes the Part of Misfortune. Uranus in the fourth shows that the end of life would come suddenly and unexpectedly. It is part of a cardinal T-square, the fulcrum of which is Neptune in the seventh house.

Pluto, ruler of the eighth house of death, is in the fifth and at almost the same degree as the lunar nodes; thus death would come through a tragic event.

The Part of Plane Crash is at 25 Cancer conjunct the South Node in the fourth, quincunx the ninth-house Moon, and opposi-

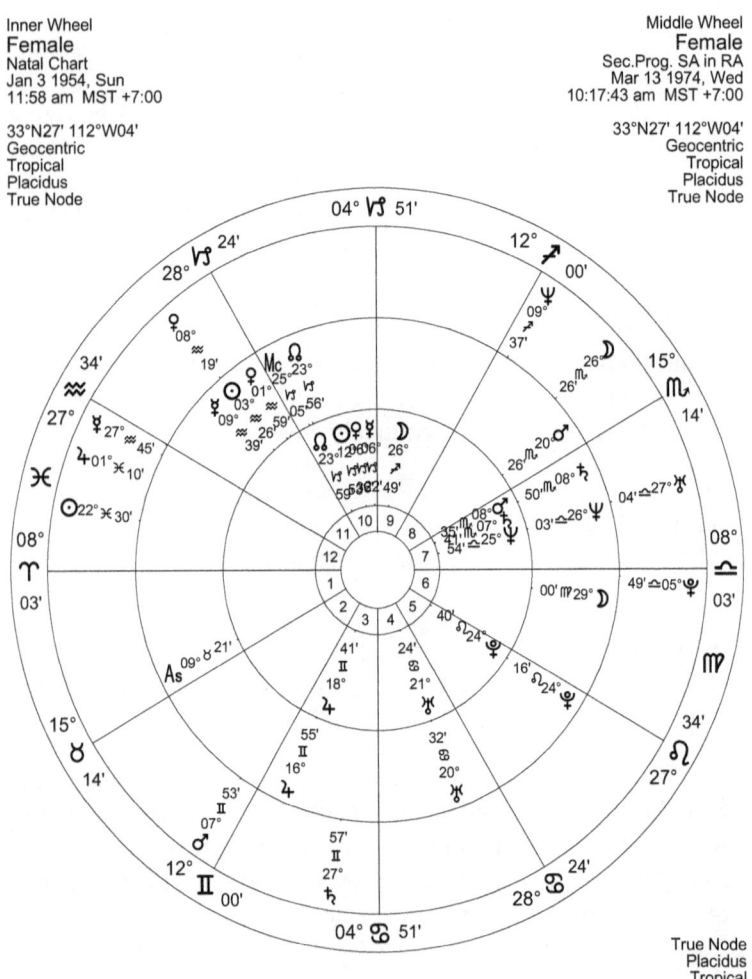

tion the Part of Peril and Pluto, with both square to Neptune. There are two Parts of Peril in this chart because Scorpio, which is on the cusp of the eighth house, has two rulers—Pluto and Mars.

Fixed Stars
- The Ascendant conjunct the fixed star Algenib (nature of Mars and Mercury).
- Markhab conjunct the Part of Fortune has the same nature as Algenib.
- Jupiter conjunct Bellatrix (nature of Mars and Mercury).
- Uranus conjunct Pollux (nature of Mars).
- Moon conjunct Acumen (nature of Mars and Moon).
- Mercury and Venus conjunct Facies (nature of Mars and Sun).

Thus we have a strong Mars emphasis throughout this chart, backing up the Aries Ascendant.

Eclipses
- January 4, 1973: a partial solar eclipse at 14 Capricorn 10, conjunct natal Sun and quincunx natal and progressed Jupiter.
- June 30, 1973: a total solar eclipse at 8 Cancer 32 opposition natal Mercury and Venus, and trine natal and progressed Mars and natal and progressed Saturn. This solar eclipse was square the natal Ascendant (physical body) and sextile the progressed Ascendant.
- December 10, 1973: a lunar eclipse at 17 Gemini 51 was conjunct natal and progressed Jupiter.
- December 24, 1973: a solar eclipse at 2 Capricorn 40 in her natal ninth house, close to the natal Midheaven.

Primary Directions
- Moon at 16 Capricorn 33, square natal Part of Plane Crash.
- Mercury and Venus both at 26 Capricorn (critical), semisextile natal Moon.

- Jupiter at 8 Cancer 17, trine natal Mars.
- Saturn at 27 Scorpio 23, semisquare natal Sun.
- Neptune at 15 Scorpio 33, conjunct natal eighth cusp.

Converse Directions
- Converse Sun at 7 Sagittarius 07, square natal Uranus, semisextile natal Saturn.
- Converse Ascendant at 18 Pisces 32, square natal Jupiter.
- Converse Mars at 18 libra 53, trine natal Jupiter.
- Converse Mercury and Venus at 16 Sagittarius, sextile natal Part of Plane Crash.
- Converse Neptune at 6 Libra 51, square natal Mercury and Venus.

Tertiary Directions

The tertiary for the event has the Part of Catastrophe conjunct the tertiary Sun, ruling the ninth house and in the tenth, both in square to natal Venus and Mercury. The Moon, ruler of the tertiary eighth house, is in the violent sign of Scorpio in wide conjunction to tertiary Mercury and Saturn, and falls in the natal eighth house, quincunx natal Jupiter. Tertiary Saturn is conjunct natal Saturn and Mars. The fixed star Caput Algol is conjunct the sixth cusp.

The tertiary Ascendant falls in opposition to natal Jupiter, with the tertiary Part of Plane Crash sitting exactly on the tertiary Ascendant, both just minutes away from a critical degree.

Tertiary Pluto, ruling the twelfth house of sorrow, straddles the tertiary ninth cusp, while Uranus, ruler of the third, is conjunct the Ascendant ruler, critical Jupiter in the eighth. In this house we also find Mars, ruler of the tertiary fourth, exactly quincunx tertiary Parts of Death and Fatality, which in turn are conjunct each other. The Part of Fortune is in exact opposition to the tertiary Uranus, and the Part of Peril is quincunx tertiary Jupiter, while Venus is besieged by Pluto and Neptune.

We can see that the emphasis here is on the same planets that were active in the natal and progressed charts at the time. The eclipses of 1973 preceding the event are very revealing of the pressures that were accumulating and show how the outside circumstances (eclipses are transits) were working to bring her to the right place at the right time for the potential of her chart to be fulfilled.

Secondary Progressions
- Progressed Ascendant semisextile natal Ascendant, opposition natal Mars, opposition progressed Saturn.
- Progressed IC conjunct natal South Node, semisextile natal and progressed Pluto.
- Progressed Sun, ruler of natal sixth of work, coworkers, and health, sesquisquare natal Jupiter, ruler of the natal ninth, conjunct natal Part of Fatality.
- Progressed Mercury critical at nine degrees of a fixed sign and sextile natal Part of Peril and Mars.
- Progressed Venus, ruler of progressed Ascendant, sesquisquare progressed Jupiter, ruler of progressed eighth, semisquare progressed Part of Death.
- Progressed Mars trine progressed Uranus.
- Progressed Part of Catastrophe trine natal Venus and Mercury.
- Progressed Moon at 25 Virgo, in March 1974, semisextile natal and progressed Neptune and progressed Part of Plane Crash, quincunx progressed Part of Peril.

Transits
- Transiting Sun in natal twelfth house conjunction natal Part of Fortune, trine progressed Mars, opposition progressed Neptune, square natal Moon, and in the tertiary third house.
- Transiting Mars quincunx natal, progressed, and tertiary Saturn; sextile natal Ascendant; semisextile progressed Ascendant; semisquare natal and progressed Uranus; quincunx natal Mercury and Venus; trine progressed Mer-

cury, conjunction progressed second cusp; trine tertiary Sun and Part of Catastrophe.
- Transiting Mercury conjunction natal twelfth cusp, conjunction natal Part of Death, trine natal and progressed Neptune, sextile natal Moon, opposition natal and progressed Pluto, sextile progressed Part of Peril, quincunx tertiary Jupiter and Uranus, opposition tertiary Pluto.
- Transiting Jupiter semisextile progressed Venus, progressed Sun, tertiary IC, and Mercury.
- Transiting Saturn in natal third house opposition the natal Moon; trine tertiary Mercury, Moon and Neptune; semisextile tertiary Jupiter and Uranus; quincunx tertiary Part of Fortune.
- Transiting Uranus retrograde conjunct natal, progressed, and tertiary Neptune; sextile natal Moon; square tertiary Jupiter and Saturn; and conjunct tertiary Moon, Mercury and Neptune.
- Transiting Venus conjunct progressed Mercury, square natal and progressed Saturn, square natal Mars, semisextile natal Venus and Mercury, square progressed Ascendant and tertiary Saturn, and sextile natal Ascendant and progressed eighth house cusp.
- Transiting Neptune trine natal Part of Peril, sextile progressed Mercury, semisquare natal and progressed Neptune.
- Transiting lunar nodes at same degree as natal and progressed Midheaven.
- Transiting Pluto square natal Mercury and Venus, semisquare progressed Mars, conjunct tertiary Sun.
- Transiting Moon in natal eighth house semisextile natal Moon; square natal Part of Death; sextile natal Part of Peril; trine natal Part of Plane Crash, progressed Uranus, and tertiary Jupiter.

Chapter 2
Hit by Car

Chris, a red-haired, freckled-face boy, already showing artistic abilities, had his share of problems during his short lifetime.

On December 8, 1967, his mother took him to the doctor because he had the flu. The doctor prescribed an injection, and when the nurse came in to give it to him, he became frightened. In the struggle that ensued, the nurse jabbed the needle into his sciatic nerve. The nerve was pinched, tissue formed around it, and the leg was crippled.

The pain was intense and on October 14, 1968 at 10:00 am, a four-hour surgery performed on his right hip left him with no feeling in the leg. Eventually the foot became twisted.

In the spring of 1969, while he was walking to school, a dog bit him on the face, but luckily no rabies was involved.

Then, in May 1971, he had corrective surgery on his heel and was awaiting further surgery to straighten his right foot. On June 10, 1971, still with a cast on his foot, Chris and his brother and two sisters were at a daycare center. A man who was intoxicated came speeding down the alley, lost control of his car and burst through the school yard fence where the children were playing. The other children scattered, but Chris could not move aside fast enough and was hit by the car. He was rushed to the hospital where he underwent surgery, but he died there of multiple head injuries.

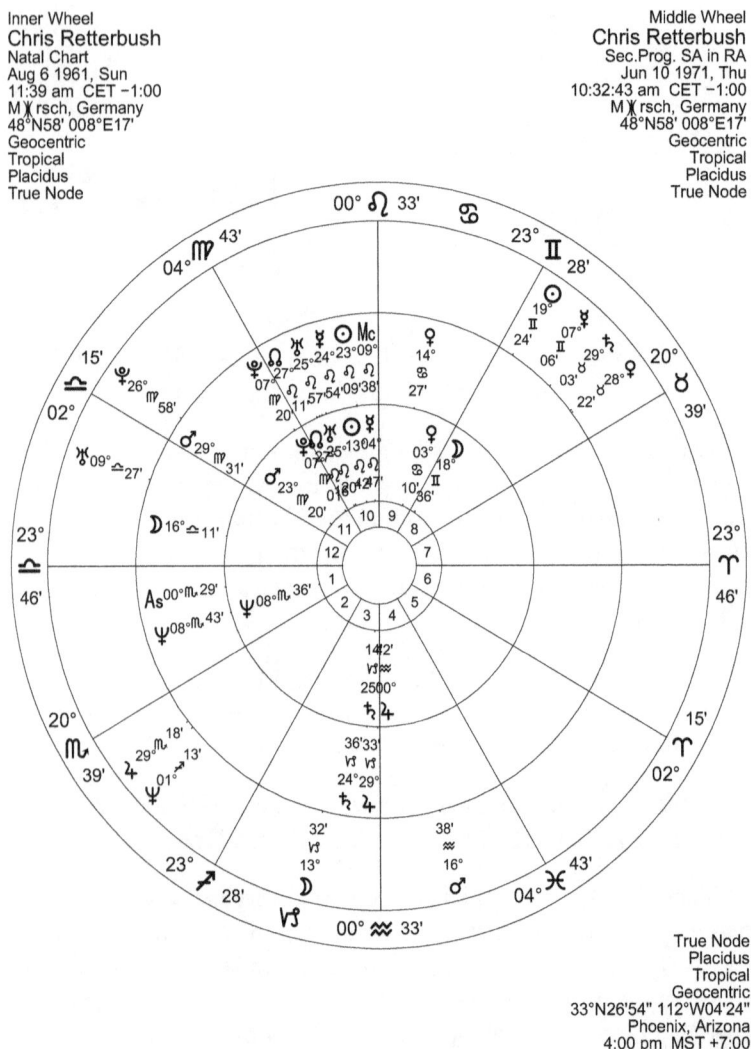

Because of the head injuries, we know that Mars, Aries, or both were involved. Chris' chart has Aries (the head) on the sixth cusp of health and, as we shall see, Mars, its ruler, was involved. The Part of Peril is critical at 0 Aries.

In the third house is a strong retrograde Saturn (an older person) co-ruling the fourth (end of life), in its own but still violent sign of Capricorn, trine the Part of Death.

The Part of Fortune is at the degree of the Nodes, while the Moon in the travel sign Gemini is semisquare Mercury, its dispositor and ruler of cars, and in the eighth house, showing that death would come to him in a public place. Venus, ruler of the Ascendant and the eighth house, is in the ninth of travel, square Part of Catastrophe in the first, stationed at the midpoint of Venus and Pluto, square Part of Fatality and trine rising Neptune; the latter is in a violent sign, Scorpio, and is the fulcrum of a fixed cross with Mercury and retrograde Jupiter.

The ruler of the ninth of travel is Mercury, which is elevated in the tenth, square the rising Neptune. It is trine Part of Fatality, square Part of Catastrophe, and at the point of outlet or manifestation for a yod.

The ruler of the other travel house, the third, is retrograde Jupiter, and in this chart is concerned with conditions at the end of life because it is exactly conjunct the fourth cusp. It is also square Neptune, semisextile Part of Peril, and opposition Mercury.

The Sun, which is life to all of us, is afflicted by the conjunction of Uranus, ruler of the fourth, and shows that the end of life would come suddenly and unexpectedly.

The seventh house of open enemies, or those who meet us head-on, is ruled by Mars in the eleventh house of circumstances beyond our control. Pluto, the Point of Accident, and Part of Death are in this house, which is Mercury-ruled with a critical degree on its cusp. Mars is sextile Point of Danger, semisextile Uranus, and also forms a semisquare to Neptune, ruler of the critical fifth cusp, and a semisextile to the Ascendant.

Fixed Stars
- Ascendant conjunct Arcturus (nature of Mars and Jupiter).
- Moon conjunct Bellatrix (nature of Mars and Mercury).
- Sun conjunct Acumens (nature of Saturn and Mercury).
- Uranus conjunct a cluster of three stars (nature of Saturn and Venus).

Thus we find a strong Mars and Saturn influence from the fixed stars.

Preceding Eclipses
- Three years before the event, Chris had a progressed solar eclipse at 18 Leo 31, semisquare natal Venus, ruler of the eighth of surgery and death, and of the Ascendant (the physical body).
- August 17, 1970, lunar eclipse at 23 Aquarius 00, quincunx natal Mars.
- August 31, 1970, solar eclipse at 8 Virgo 04, conjunct natal and progressed Pluto.
- February 10, 1971, lunar eclipse critical at 21 Leo, conjunct progressed Sun, square Point of Danger, semisextile natal Mars.
- The last eclipse to occur before the event was a solar eclipse at 6 Pisces 00, opposition natal and progressed Pluto, trine natal and progressed Neptune.

Primary Directions
- Saturn at 4 Aquarius 57, opposition natal Mercury, semi-square natal Moon.
- Jupiter at 9 Aquarius quincunx the Point of Accident.

Converse Directions
- Converse Ascendant at 13 libra 22, critical, sextile natal Sun.
- Converse Moon at 8 Gemini 55, quincunx Neptune, sesquisquare natal Ascendant.
- Converse Sun at 4 Leo 54, conjunct natal Mercury, square natal Part of Catastrophe.
- Converse Mars at 13 Virgo 39, semisextile natal Sun.
- Converse Venus at 23 Gemini 28, trine natal Ascendant, square Mars, sesquisquare Neptune, quincunx Point of Danger.
- Converse Uranus at 15 Leo 39, sesquisquare natal Part of Peril.
- Converse Pluto at 27 Leo 18, conjunct North Node.

Tertiary Directions

The tertiary directions for June 10, 1971 were:

- Tertiary Ascendant in natal fourth house (end of life), semisquare natal Part of Fatality, quincunx tertiary Part of Death.
- Tertiary Uranus, ruler of tertiary Ascendant, retrograde and conjunct tertiary Pluto in tertiary seventh, quincunx Jupiter, quincunx natal Part of Peril.
- Tertiary Saturn conjunct natal lunar Nodes and in violent Capricorn, conjunct natal Saturn.
- Tertiary Sun and Mars conjunct tertiary Mercury, all three conjunct natal ninth cusp, square natal Mars, semisextile natal Point of Danger, opposition natal eighth-house Moon.
- Tertiary Neptune in tertiary eighth square natal Sun.
- Tertiary fifth and eleventh cusps critical at 0 cardinal.
- Tertiary Pluto square tertiary Venus, opposition tertiary Moon, conjunct radix Point of Accident, sesquisquare natal and progressed Saturn.

- Tertiary Moon critical in tertiary first, square tertiary four-planet stellium in transportation sign Sagittarius, square the natal Moon.
- Tertiary Jupiter sesquiquadrate tertiary Mercury, sextile tertiary Venus, square radix and tertiary Neptune.
- Tertiary Venus in tertiary ninth house trine radix Sun, sesquisquare radix Fortuna, opposition natal Moon.
- Tertiary Part of Fortune square radix Sun.
- Tertiary Part of Fatality opposition natal Part of Death and Mars, sesquiquadrate natal Neptune.
- Tertiary Part of Peril opposition natal Venus, square radix Part of Fatality, sextile natal Part of Catastrophe.
- Tertiary Part of Catastrophe same degree as natal Nodes, trine tertiary Saturn, semisextile natal Part of Fortune.

Secondary Progressions
- Progressed Midheaven critical at 9 degrees fixed.
- Progressed Ascendant square natal Mercury (outlet for yod), conjunct natal Part of Catastrophe.
- Progressed Venus, ruler of both Ascendants and natal eighth house critcal at 13 degrees cardinal, square progressed Part of Fatality (also critical), semisextile natal Sun, trine progressed Part of Catastrophe.
- Progressed Mars at 29 degrees (out of rope) trine progressed Jupiter, semisquare progressed Part of Catastrophe.
- Progressed Mercury, ruler of progressed eighth, semisextile natal Mars, square Point of Danger.
- Progressed Part of Death square natal Venus.
- Progressed Moon for June 1971 at 4 libra 39 sextile natal Mercury, semisextile natal Ascendant and natal Part of Catastrophe, opposition natal Part of Fatality.
- Part of Fortune for June 1971 semisextile progressed Ascendant, trine radix Mercury, square natal and progressed Pluto, quincunx natal Venus, trine natal Part of Fatality, semisextile natal Part of Catastrophe.

Transits

The transits for June 10, 1971 were:

- Transiting Sun conjunct natal Moon in natal eighth, opposition tertiary Mercury, Sun, and Mars.
- Transiting Venus at same degree as natal lunar Nodes, trine progressed Mars, square natal and progressed Uranus, square natal Part of Fortune, trine tertiary Part of Catastrophe and Saturn.
- Transiting Saturn conjunct transiting Venus in natal eighth, trine progressed Mars, trine natal and progressed Jupiter, square natal lunar Nodes and part of Fortune, trine teritiary Part of Peril and Saturn.
- Transiting Mercury quincunx natal Part of Catastrophe, sextile natal Part of Fatality, square natal and progressed Pluto, sesquisquare natal Ascendant, quincux progressed Ascendant, trine tertiary Jupiter.
- Transiting Pluto trine natal and progressed Jupiter, semisquare natal Sun, semisextile natal Part of Fortune, trine tertiary Saturn, conjunct tertiary Part of Catastrophe.
- Transiting retrograde Uranus semisquare natal Point of Danger and natal and progressed Uranus, semisextile natal and progressed Neptune.
- Transiting retrograde Jupiter at 29 degrees (out of rope), sesquisquares progressed Part of Fatality, square natal Part of Fortune, sextile tertiary Saturn.
- Transiting retrograde Neptune quincunx natal Venus, sextile natal Jupiter, trine natal Mercury, in tertiary ninth house.
- Transiting Mars opposition natal Sun, trine natal Moon, square progressed Part of Catastrophe, sextile progressed Part of Fatality, conjunct tertiary Ascendant.
- Transiting Moon, timer of the event, critical at 13 degrees cardinal in Capricorn (violence), in natal third, quincunx natal Sun, square progressed Part of Fatality, sextile tertiary

Neptune, sextile progressed Part of Catastrophe, conjunct progressed Venus, sesquisquare natal Part of Fortune. These aspects fulfilled this chart's potential.

Chapter 3

Hit by Train

This first chart is the son of one of my students, and the other is her father and the son's grandfather. Both were instantly killed when their car was struck by a train at a crossing.

Son/Grandson

There are many important factors here, but three of them really stand out. The first is retrograde, detrimented Mars, ruling the fifth (recklessness) and co-ruling the twelfth (hidden things), straddling the sixth of health, and semisquare the Point of Accident.

The second is retrograde Uranus, ruler of the travel third and fulcrum of a fixed T-square with Mars and Jupiter. Uranus is on the cusp of the travel ninth (trains go long distances) like a vulture biding its time, semisquare the Point of Accident.

The third is the five-planet stellium in Sagittarius, sign of transportation, in the personal first house. Mercury rises in the chart, also retrograde and detrimented, conjunct Part of Peril and representing his maternal grandfather.

The Moon is in the first house (along with the stellium) conjunct Saturn. It is detrimented in violent Capricorn, and is critical at zero degrees cardinal. It rules the eighth house and is besieged by Mars and Saturn; the latter, ruling trains, is also the dispositor of the Moon.

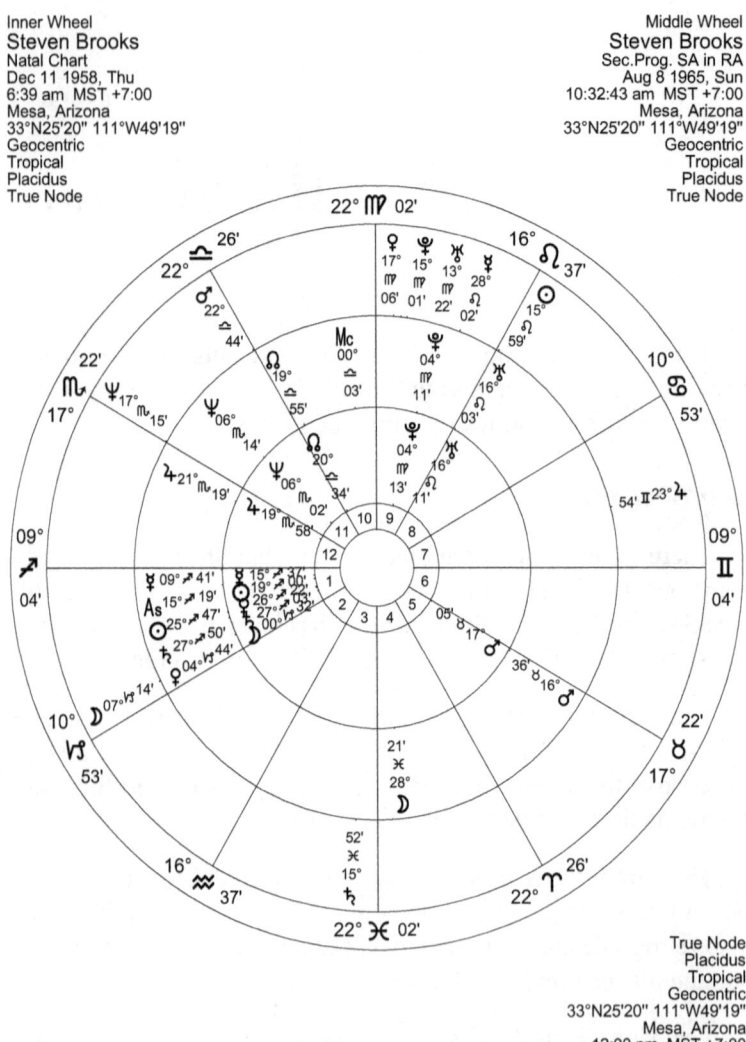

The Moon is in opposition to the Point of Accident, sesquisquare Mars and Uranus, and trine the ninth-house Pluto, which in turn rules the twelfth of sorrows, and is retrograde and square the Ascendant.

Jupiter, the greater benefic, rules the Ascendant (the physical body) and is at the same degree as the lunar Nodes and conjunct Serpentis at the cursed degree of the cursed sign in violent Scorpio; it disposits the Sagittarius stellium and thus cannot help.

Neptune is also in violent Scorpio (and note here that its degree is Steven's age at the time of the fatal accident). It rules the fourth house (end of life), is square Part of Plane Crash in the eighth, and also at six degrees.

The Sun, ruling the travel ninth, is in the first as part of the stellium, and exactly opposition Part of Death. It is conjunct the Part of Fortune and, like Jupiter, is at the same degree as the lunar Nodes. Venus, the lesser benefic, in the first house afflicted by its conjunction to Saturn, and so cannot help him either. It is semisextile/quincunx the Antivertex/Vertex.

Fixed Stars
- Ascendant conjunct Antares (nature of Mars and Jupiter).
- Saturn conjunct Acumen (nature of Mars and Moon).
- Mercury conjunct Sabik (nature of Saturn and Venus).
- Neptune conjunct Khamvalia (nature of Mercury and Mars).

Preceding Eclipses
- June 10, 1964, partial solar eclipse at 18 Gemini 19, opposition natal Sun, conjunct natal Part of Death.
- June 25, 1964, total lunar eclipse at 3 Capricorn 18, trine natal and progressed Pluto.
- July 9, 1964, partial solar eclipse at 17 Cancer 14, sextile natal and progressed Mars, semisextile natal and pro-

gressed Uranus.
- December 4, 1964, partial solar eclipse at 11 Sagittarius 56, conjunct natal Ascendant, natal Part of Peril, and natal Mercury; semisquare critical Antivertex degree (physical manifestation).
- December 19, 1964, total lunar eclipse at 27 Gemini 00, opposition natal Venus, opposition natal and progressed Saturn.
- May 30, 1965, total solar eclipse at 9 Gemini 13, conjunct natal Ascendant, opposition natal Ascendant and retrograde progressed Mercury, square natal Point of Danger.
- June 14, 1965, partial lunar eclipse at 22 Sagittarius 30, semisquare natal and progressed Neptune, conjunct natal Fortuna and progressed Part of Fatality.

Primary Directions
- Ascendant at 13 Sagittarius 56, conjunct natal Mercury.
- Saturn at 3 Capricorn 57, trine natal Pluto.
- Neptune at 12 Scorpio 37, semisquare natal Saturn.
- Jupiter at 26 Scorpio 33, semisextile natal Venus.
- Part of Peril at 19 Sagittarius 55, conjunct natal Sun, opposition natal Part of Death, semisextile natal Jupiter, same degree as the natal lunar Nodes.
- Part of Plane Crash at 14 Leo 01, trine natal Part of Peril.
- Part of Death at 26 Gemini 26, opposition natal Venus.

Converse Directions
- Converse Mercury at 9 Sagittarius 58, retrograde, conjunct natal Ascendant.
- Converse Jupiter at 13 Scorpio 25, semisextile natal Part of Peril.
- Converse Uranus at 09 Leo 38, critical degree.
- Converse Venus at 19 Sagittarius 49, conjunct natal Sun.

Tertiary Directions

The tertiary directions were also very drastic.

- Scorpio, a violent sign, rises, square natal Part of Catastrophe, with its ruler Pluto at the critical 13 degrees cardinal, exactly conjunct the tertiary twelfth cusp, which is also critical. Pluto is sextile natal Part of Peril, falling on natal Neptune.
- There is a five-planet stellium with four of the planets in the personal first house, while Neptune, the fifth planet, is conjunct the tertiary Ascendant from the twelfth house, all in Scorpio (violence).
- Rising Venus is critical at nine degrees fixed and detrimented, and square the tertiary Midheaven, Moon, and Part of Catastrophe.
- The tertiary Moon is in the tertiary ninth house, which it rules, square the tertiary Sun and the entire tertiary stellium, and in the natal eighth house conjunct natal Uranus.
- Tertiary Jupiter's conjunction to tertiary Sun is no help because it is square natal and tertiary Uranus.
- Tertiary Mars, retrograde and detrimented (like natal Mars), ruling the critical tertiary sixth cusp and co-ruling the tertiary Ascendant, opposes tertiary Mercury, is quincunx natal Saturn, and conjunct the fixed star cluster the Pleiades (something to cry about).
- Tertiary Mercury, ruling the tertiary Eighth, can no longer function, being at 29 degrees in opposition to the Pleiades.
- Tertiary Uranus is back at the degree of natal Uranus (now direct—no more holding back) and still the fulcrum of a fixed T-square, this time with tertiary Mercury and Mars.
- Tertiary Saturn, ruler of the tertiary fourth (end of life), is semisquare rising tertiary Venus, trine natal and tertiary Uranus, and square natal Midheaven and I.C.
- Tertiary Venus sextile natal Ascendant.
- Tertiary Neptune semisquare natal Sun.

- Tertiary Part of Death conjunct natal and tertiary Pluto.
- Tertiary Part of Fatality conjunct natal Sun.
- Tertiary Fortuna square natal Neptune and tertiary Ascendant.

Secondary Progressions
- Progressed Ascendant conjunct natal Part of Peril, trine progressed Part of Catastrophe.
- Progressed Mercury, retrograde, conjunct natal Ascendant.
- Progressed Venus trine natal and progressed Pluto.
- Retrograde progressed Mars completed its square to natal Uranus and the natal ninth cusp, quincunx natal Part of Fatality.
- Progressed Jupiter, now retrograde, had been at the critical 21 degrees, fixed, for a couple of years.
- Progressed Moon for July 1965 at 26 Pisces 36, square natal Venus and progressed Part of Death, and trine/sextile Vertex/Antivertex.
- The Part of Fortune at 15 Gemini opposition natal Mercury.

Transits
- Transiting Sun conjunct natal, progressed, and tertiary Uranus and natal ninth cusp; square natal and progressed Mars; trine natal Part of Fatality; trine natal Mercury; sesquisquare natal Moon and natal fourth cusp.
- Transiting Mercury, retrograde, trine natal and progressed Venus and Saturn; square tertiary Mars and Mercury.
- Transiting Uranus, Pluto, and Venus (conjunct in Virgo) in natal ninth house; square natal first house stellium and progressed Ascendant; conjunct tertiary eleventh cusp (no hopes for the future); semisextile tertiary Pluto and twelfth cusp of sorrows; square natal Part of Peril; quincunx tertiary fourth cusp; sextile tertiary Sun and Jupiter.
- Transiting Mars, detrimented, semisquare natal Point of Danger; conjunct natal eleventh cusp; square natal Venus

and Saturn; sextile progressed Part of Fatality and Sun; semisextile progressed Jupiter; trine progressed Part of Death.
- Transiting Neptune conjunct natal twelfth cusp and Jupiter; opposition natal and progressed Mars; square natal, progressed, and tertiary Uranus; in tertiary first house.
- Transiting retrograde Saturn square natal Mercury, Sun, and Part of Fatality; in natal third house; sextile natal and progressed Mars; quincunxe natal, progressed, and tertiary Uranus; conjunct tertiary fifth cusp; square progressed Ascendant.
- Transiting Jupiter opposition natal Venus, natal Saturn and progressed Part of Fatality; square progressed Midheaven and IC; opposition tertiary Saturn; square progressed Moon; opposition natal Fortuna.

The pressures were very great and, with so much activity in the fixed signs, there was no avoiding the potential of this chart.

Father/Grandfather

Violent Capricorn rises in this chart, with Mars conjunct Venus, also in Capricorn, rising in the first house. Mars rules the fourth house (end of life), while Venus is sextile Saturn, with these planets ruling the tenth (line of destiny) and fifth, the cusp of the latter being conjunct the fixed star Caput Algol.

In the first house we find Fortuna, which saved him for many years. Mercury, also in the first and ruler of the ninth, is retrograde in Aquarius, and square and disposited by Uranus, which is conjunct Saturn in the tenth house, both in violent Scorpio. Saturn rules the Ascendant and is square the Vertex/Antivertex, while Uranus is square the Sun, ruler of the eighth house.

The Moon, ruler of the public seventh house, is conjunct the North Node at the critical four degrees, mutable. It is square Pluto and Neptune, and trine Part of Peril and Part of Fatality.

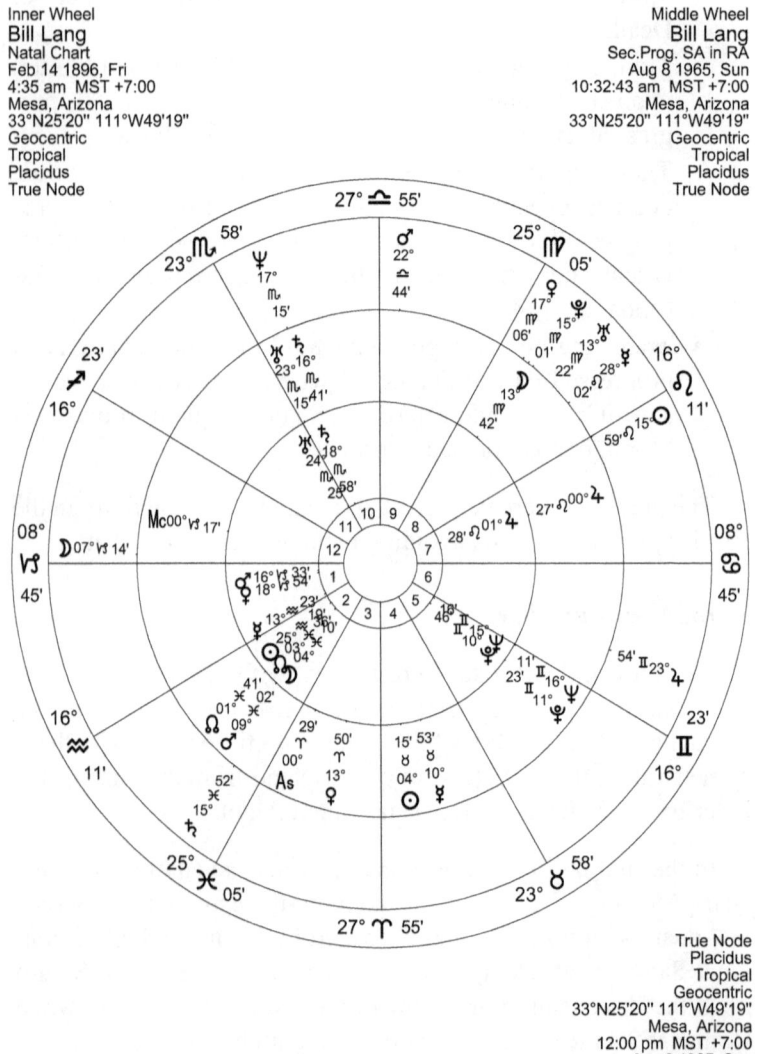

Neptune, ruling the travel third, is conjunct Pluto. Both are retrograde in transportation Gemini, quincunx the rising Mars-Venus conjunction, and opposition the Point of Danger and the Point of Accidents.

Retrograde Jupiter is in the seventh house, ruling the twelfth of hidden things and co-ruling the travel third. It is quincunx the critical Moon and its North Node conjunction, and sextiJe Part of Fatality and Part of Peril.

Fixed Stars
- Venus conjunct Deneb (nature of Mars and Jupiter).
- Mercury conjunct Dorsum (nature of Saturn and Jupiter).
- Neptune conjunct Rigel (nature of Jupiter and Mars).

Preceding Eclipses
- July 9, 1964, partial solar eclipse at 17 Cancer 14, in natal seventh house, opposition natal Mars and Venus, trine natal Saturn.
- December 4, 1964, partial solar eclipse at 11 Sagittarius 56, opposition natal Neptune and Pluto, conjunct natal Point of Danger.
- May 30, 1965, total solar eclipse at 9 Gemini 13, conjunct natal Pluto, quincunx natal Ascendant, trine natal Part of Catastrophe.
- June 14, 1965, partial lunar eclipse at 22 Sagittarius 30, conjunct natal Point of Accident in natal twelfth.

Primary Directions
- Ascendant at 17 Pisces 35, critical.
- Mars at 25 Pisces 05, semisextile natal Sun.
- Mercury at 21 Aries 54, square natal Fortuna.
- Neptune at 23 Leo 27, semisquare natal Part of Catastrophe.
- Jupiter at 10 Libra 00, sesquisquare natal Sun.
- Uranus at 2 Aquarius 57, trine natal Part of Peril.

- Part of Catastrophe at 16 Sagittarius 42, almost to the critical degree, semisextile natal Mars, square natal Jupiter.
- Part of Peril at 15 Sagittarius 00, opposition natal Neptune.
- Midheaven at 6 Capricorn 30, square natal Part of Peril.

Converse Directions
- Converse Ascendant at 00 Scorpio 35, sesquisquare natal radlx Neptune.
- Converse Mars at 8 Scorpio 15, semisextile natal Part of Catastrophe.
- Converse Venus at 10 Scorpio 26, semiquare natal ninth cusp, sesquisquare natal third cusp.
- Converse Mercury at 4 Sagittarius 54, critical, square natal Moon and lunar Nodes.
- Converse Sun at 16 Sagittarius 50, semisextile natal Mars, sesquisquare natal Jupiter.
- Converse Moon at 25 Sagittarius 55, sextile natal Sun, sesquisquare natal Neptune.
- Converse Pluto at 2 Aries 17, opposition natal Part of Fatality.
- Converse Neptune at 6 Aries 47, opposition natal Part of Peril.
- Converse Uranus at 15 Virgo 57, square natal Neptune.

Tertiary Directions
- Tertiary Ascendant in natal eighth house, square natal Saturn.
- Tertiary Part of Death critical at 21 degrees fixed, conjunct tertiary Ascendant, square natal Uranus, quincunx natal Fortuna.
- Tertiary Part of Fatality in tertiary third, sextile natal Mars and Venus, semisquare natal Part of Fatality.
- Tertiary Part of Catastrophe, also in tertiary third, trine tertiary Moon and Peril Neptune, quincunx natal Neptune.

- Tertiary Sun, ruler tertiary Ascendant, in tertiary first, opposition tertiary Moon and Peril Neptune (there are two Parts of Peril in this chart because of Pisces on the eighth cusp).
- Tertiary Sun semisquare natal Uranus and semisextile natal Part of Catastrophe
- Tertiary Pluto in Gemini, rules tertiary fourth, conjunct natal Neptune, opposition natal Point of Danger.
- Tertiary Uranus, retrograde at 29 degrees of violent Scorpio, in tertiary fourth, sesquisquare natal Moon and North Node.
- Tertiary Saturn, retrograde in tertiary fourth, square tertiary Sun and Moon, opposition tertiary Pluto, quincunx natal Part of Peril.
- Tertiary Mercury critical at 17 degrees mutable, opposition tertiary Moon, square tertiary Pluto, sextile tertiary Part of Fatality, sextile natal Neptune and Saturn, semisextile natal Mars and Venus.
- Tertiary Venus in tertiary third, ruler third, square natal Fortuna, trine tertiary Mars, semisquare tertiary Sun, sesquisquare tertiary Peril Neptune.
- Tertiary Mars, ruler tertiary ninth, quincunx tertiary Uranus, conjunct tertiary Neptune and Peril Jupiter, sesquisquare natal Mercury.
- Tertiary Neptune ruler tertiary eighth, conjunct tertiary Peril Jupiter, sextile natal Uranus.
- Tertiary Jupiter, co-ruler tertiary eighth, conjunct tertiary third cusp, coniunct natal Part of Catastrophe, trine natal Pluto.

Secondary Progressions

- Progressed Ascendant opposition natal Part of Peril.
- Progressed fourth cusp same degree as natal lunar Nodes, trine natal Moon.
- Progressed Mercury, critical at nine degrees fixed, trine na-

tal Ascendant.
- Progressed Venus, critical at 13 degrees cardinal, semisquare progressed Mars, sesquisquare progressed Uranus, sextile natal Mercury, trine the natal Point of Danger.
- Progressed Pluto conjunct progressed third cusp of travel, opposition progressed Part of Fatality.
- Progressed Part of Catastrope semisextile natal Mars, semisextile progressed Saturn.
- Progressed Part of Peril semisquare progressed Jupiter, opposition natal Neptune.
- Progressed Moon, July, at 28 Leo 38, sesquisquare progressed Venus, square progressed Uranus, semisextile natal Mars/Pluto.
- Progressed Part of Fortune, July, at 1 Leo 27, conjunct natal Jupiter, semisquare progressed Neptune, sesquisquare progressed Part of Catastrophe, semisextile Neptune/Saturn.

Transits

- Transiting Sun conjunct natal eighth cusp, square natal Saturn, opposition natal Mercury, quincunx natal Mars, sextile natal Neptune, trine progressed Part of Peril and Venus, sextile tertiary Pluto, square tertiary Midheaven and IC.
- Transiting Venus, retrograde, square natal Uranus, sesquisquare progressed Venus, sextile tertiary Mars and Uranus.
- Transiting Uranus, Venus and Pluto (all three conjunct in Virgo in natal eighth house) square the Point of Danger, trine natal Mars and Venus, square natal and progressed Neptune, quincunx natal Mercury, conjunct tertiary second cusp, opposition tertiary eighth cusp; Venus and Pluto at same degree as tertiary lunar Nodes.
- Transiting Mars square natal Fortuna, trine natal Sun, sextile Point of Accident, semisextile natal Uranus and tertiary Sun, conjunct tertiary Venus, sesquisquare tertiary Part of Peril Neptune.

- Transiting Neptune conjunct natal Neptune and tertiary Part of Fatality, sextile natal Mars and Venus, sextile progressed Part of Peril and Part of Catastrophe, sextile tertiary Mercury, semisquare natal Part of Fatality, quincunx progressed Neptune.
- Transiting lunar Nodes at the same degree as natal Mars, progressed Saturn and Neptune, with the South Node conjunct progressed Neptune.
- Transiting Saturn trine natal and progressed Saturn, square Point of Danger, square natal and progressed Neptune, square tertiary Pluto, sextile natal Mars and Venus, opposition tertiary Mercury, conjunct tertiary Moon.
- Transiting Jupiter quincunx natal Uranus and Fortuna, conjunct tertiary Jupiter, sextile tertiary Part of Death, trine tertiary Venus.
- Transiting Moon trine progressed Sun and Mercury, quincunx natal Jupiter and progressed Fortuna, square progressed Ascendant, semisquare progressed Saturn.

As we compare this chart with Steven's chart we see that the boy's Uranus and ninth cusp are conjunct his grandfather's eighth cusp, while Mars is square it.

Bill's Point of Danger is conjunct Steven's Part of Peril, Bill's Point of Accident is conjunct Steven's Sun and Fortuna, and Steven's Pluto is close to Bill's South Node in the eighth house. Bill's Saturn is conjunct Steven's Jupiter and twelfth house cusp, Steven's Part of Fatality and Mercury are conjunct Bill's twelfth cusp.

Thus the two charts were linked for the shared tragedy.

Chapter 4

Head-on Car Collision

On 15 May 1965, my parents, who then resided in Verdun, Canada, decided to drive to their summer camp in the Laurentians to enjoy the spring weather and to air out the camp for the coming summer.

They were halfway to their destination when a taxicab with driver and male passenger came speeding around a curve at eighty miles per hour. Because of the speed the cab driver lost control of his car, crossed over to the wrong side of the road, and crashed headlong into my parents' car at approximately 12:10 pm at latitude 46N.

My dad, the cab driver, and his passenger were killed instantly. But my mother, who had been dozing, survived.

This is the summation of my dad's injuries: Death was due to a cerebral hemorrhage (Mars influence and Aries Ascendant). Left arm broken, chest crushed with ribs shattered (Mercury influence; Mars, Pluto, and Neptune in Gemini). Left hip broken (Jupiter and Sagittarius influence) and left ankle broken (Uranus).

In his chart, violent Aries rises. Mars, its ruler (co-ruler of the eighth house) is conjunct the South Node, sextile Fortuna and Mercury, quincunx the Moon, opposition Uranus, semisextile the fourth cusp, and square the Point of Accident and Part of Catastrophe.

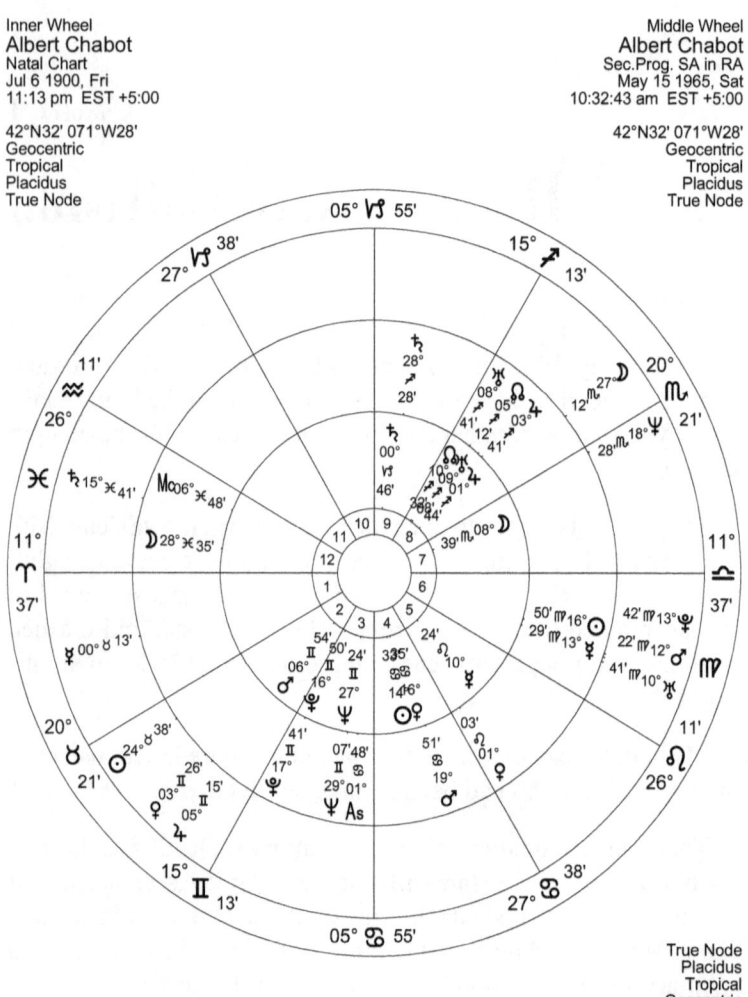

The Moon in the seventh house of partners and open enemies in violent Scorpio is square Mercury and sextile the fourth-house Sun and Venus. The Moon also rules the end-of-life fourth house.

Saturn is in the ninth of travel and foreign countries. It is strong in its own sign, violent Capricorn (critical), quincunx Mars and Fortuna, and semisextile Jupiter.

Uranus is conjunct the South Node in the eighth house. It is trine Mercury, sesquisquare Part of Death in the first house, and semisquare the Point of Danger.

Mercury, ruler of the third, is sextile Pluto from the fifth house of pleasure, while Pluto in travel Gemini in the third is conjunct the third cusp, bringing danger from the left side of the road. Pluto is square the critical Peril Mars and semisquare Peril Pluto.

Neptune is also in Gemini in the third, square Peril Pluto and Part of Fatality. The Point of Danger is square Neptune and semisquare Fortuna.

All parts, Catastrophe, Points of Accident and Danger, Fatality, Peril Mars and Peril Pluto are grouped together in Virgo in the sixth house of work and health. The sixth is also his wife's twelfth house of hospitals.

Jupiter is also in the eighth house of death conjunct the North Node and Uranus. It is strong in its own sign of Sagittarius (ruling foreign countries), opposition Mars, sesquisquare retrograde Mercury in the fourth, and trine Fortuna.

Fixed Stars
- Pluto conjunct Rigel (nature of Jupiter and Mars).
- Neptune conjunct Betelgeuse (nature of Mars and Mercury).
- Sun and Venus conjunct Canopus (nature of Saturn and Jupiter); conjunct Sirius (nature of Jupiter and Mars).
- Jupiter conjunct Yed Prior (nature of Saturn and Venus).

- Saturn conjunct Spiculum (nature of Mars and Moon).
- Uranus and North Node conjunct Antares (nature of Mars and Jupiter).

Preceding Eclipses
- June 10, 1964, partial solar eclipse at 19 Gemini 19, conjunct natal and progressed Pluto.
- June 25, 1964, total lunar eclipse at 3 Capricorn 18, conjunct natal Saturn and Midheaven, quincunx natal Mars.
- July 4, 1964, partial solar eclipse at 17 Capricorn 14, opposition natal Sun and Venus, trine natal Peril Mars, quincunx natal and progressed Pluto, conjunct progressed Mars.
- December 4, 1964, partial solar eclipse at 11 Sagittarius 54 conjunct natal and progressed Uranus, trine natal Ascendant, square progressed Sun, Mercury, Midheaven, and IC.
- December 19, 1964, total lunar eclipse at 27 Gemini 00, conjunct natal and progressed Neptune.

Primary Directions
- Ascendant at to 15 Gemini 50, conjunct the natal third cusp.
- Mars at 10 Leo 29, conjunct natal Mercury.
- Neptune at 1 Virgo 18, square natal Jupiter.
- Sun at 10 Virgo 00, semisextile natal Mercury.
- Mercury at 13 Libra 55, critical, cardinal degree.
- Jupiter at 27 Leo 52, sextile natal Neptune, semisextile natal Peril Pluto.
- Saturn at 4 Pisces 44, critical, mutable degree.
- Fourth cusp at 9 Virgo 55, square natal Uranus at same degree as natal lunar Nodes.
- Part of Death at 27 Gemini 53, conjunct natal Neptune, square natal Peril Pluto.
- Peril Mars at 21 Scorpio 31, critical, fixed degree in a violent sign, sesquisquare natal fourth cusp.
- Peril Pluto at 1 Sagittarius 35, sesquisquare natal Venus.

Converse Directions
- Converse Ascendant at 7 Aquarius 59, square natal Moon, quincunx Point of Accident.
- Converse Neptune at 23 Aries 28, semisquare natal Neptune.
- Converse Mercury at 6 Gemini 05, conjunct natal Mars.
- Converse Moon at 4 Virgo 46, critical, mutable degree.
- Converse Jupiter at 27 Virgo 52, square natal Neptune, conjunct natal Peril Pluto.
- Converse Saturn at 26 Libra 54, critical, cardinal degree.
- Converse Midheaven at 2 Scorpio 45, semisquare natal Point of Accident.
- Converse Part of Fatality at 24 Cancer 40, sesquisquare natal Uranus and North Node.
- Peril Pluto at 23 Cancer 45, square natal Part of Death.

Tertiary Directions
- Tertiary Ascendant at fatal 29 degrees, semisquare natal Sun.
- Tertiary Sun in natal ninth, rules tertiary Ascendant, in tertiary fourth (in Sagittarius of travel and foreign countries), opposition retrograde Pluto, ruler of tertiary Fourth, trine tertiary Part of Death.
- Tertiary Venus, ruler of tertiary third, in tertiary fourth, semisextile tertiary Saturn in fifth of pleasure, quincunx natal Fortuna, at the degree of the tertiary lunar Nodes, in the natal eighth House.
- Tertiary Saturn, in violent Capricorn, at same degree as tertiary nodes, square natal Part of Death, opposition tertiary Moon.
- Tertiary Moon semisextile tertiary Ascendant (then void of course), in tertiary eleventh of hopes and wishes, sextile natal Part of Fatality and Peril Pluto.
- Tertiary Neptune, retrograde, square tertiary Part of Fatality and Fortuna in tertiary eighth house.

- Tertiary Mars in tertiary first, rules tertiary ninth, semisquare tertiary Moon, square natal and tertiary Pluto; fulcrum of a mutable T-square.
- Tertiary Peril Jupiter conjunct natal Peril Mars and tertiary Mars, sextile natal Sun.
- Tertiary Mercury in tertiary third, trine natal Sun and Venus. Tertiary Jupiter opposition natal Mercury, sextile natal Uranus, square tertiary Mercury, co-ruler tertiary eighth, conjunct tertiary Peril Neptune.
- Tertiary Peril Neptune sextile natal Uranus and South Node.
- Tertiary Fortuna in tertiary eighth, opposition tertiary Part of Fatality, sextile tertiary Jupiter, square natal fourth cusp, trine natal Fortuna.

Secondary Progressions

- Progressed Ascendant same degree as progressed lunar Nodes for a personal loss (in this case, his life).
- Progressed Venus semisquare progressed Sun.
- Progressed Mercury semisextile natal Mercury, quincunx natal Ascendant, sextile progressed Part of Catastrophe.
- Progressed fourth cusp sextile natal Moon, square progressed Uranus.
- Progressed Moon, May, at 17 Pisces 44, critical degree, opposition natal Peril Mars, square progressed Pluto.
- Progressed Fortuna, May, at 7 Capricorn 54, trine natal Point of Accident, semisquare progressed critical Peril Mars.

Transits

The accident occurred during a Full Moon in violent Scorpio. (Dad was a Cancer.) The transits for the day of the event were:

- Transiting Sun trine Point of Danger, trine tertiary Saturn,

opposition tertiary Venus, conjunct tertiary Midheaven, opposition tertiary fourth cusp at same degree as tertiary lunar Nodes.
- Transiting Venus opposition progressed Part of Fatality and natal and progressed Jupiter, semisquare progressed Mars.
- Transiting Jupiter conjunct natal Mars, square natal Part of Catastrophe, opposition natal Uranus, conjunct progressed South Node, semisquare progressed Mars, sextile tertiary Fortuna.
- Transiting lunar Nodes same degree as natal Sun, semisquare tertiary Moon.
- Transiting Uranus, Mars, and Pluto stellium in Virgo conjunct progressed fourth cusp, Mercury, Sun, and tertiary Mars; sextile natal Sun; opposition progressed Moon; semisquare progressed Venus.
- Transiting Neptune in violent Scorpio quincunx natal and progressed Pluto, sextile natal Peril Mars, semisquare tertiary Part of Fatality.
- Transiting Saturn conjunct progressed Moon; opposition natal Peril Mars, progressed Sun, and Mercury; square natal and progressed Pluto; trine natal Sun and progressed Mars; opposition tertiary Mars and Peril Jupiter.
- Transiting Moon in natal eighth house conjunct progressed Peril Mars, sextile tertiary Saturn, conjunct tertiary Venus, at the same degree as tertiary lunar Nodes.

Chapter 5

Hit by Car

On June 26, 1971, this young man was out for an evening of pleasure (fifth house) with friends (eleventh house). The car would not start, so he and his friends were pushing it when another young man drove into them at approximately 8:45 pm. The only one who was injured was the owner of the above chart, although the driver of the other car had a broken nose.

Our young man had his hip decapitated—Caput Algol on the Ascendant, Jupiter ruling the hip—and he died in the hospital at 11:00 pm DST, 34N, as the transiting Moon reached 21 Leo, critical. No attempt had been made to stop the hemorrhaging (afflicted Jupiter). The strain on the heart was too great (Pluto in Leo in fourth) and the coroner's report read, "tear in the heart." The Ascendant of this chart is between two fixed stars—Caput Algol of the nature of Saturn and Jupiter, symbolic of decapitation, and Capulus of the nature of Mars and Mercury. The Ascendant is square the Part of Fatality and is in the third of travel.

Venus, ruler of the chart, is rising in the transportation sign of Gemini, and is the fulcrum of a mutable T-square with Jupiter and Saturn. Also trine Neptune, Venus is sextile Pluto in the fourth (end of life).

Jupiter rules the eighth and is in the eleventh of friends, which it co-rules. It is retrograde, conjunct the Part of Misfortune (Fortuna in Pisces), in opposition to Saturn in the fifth of plea-

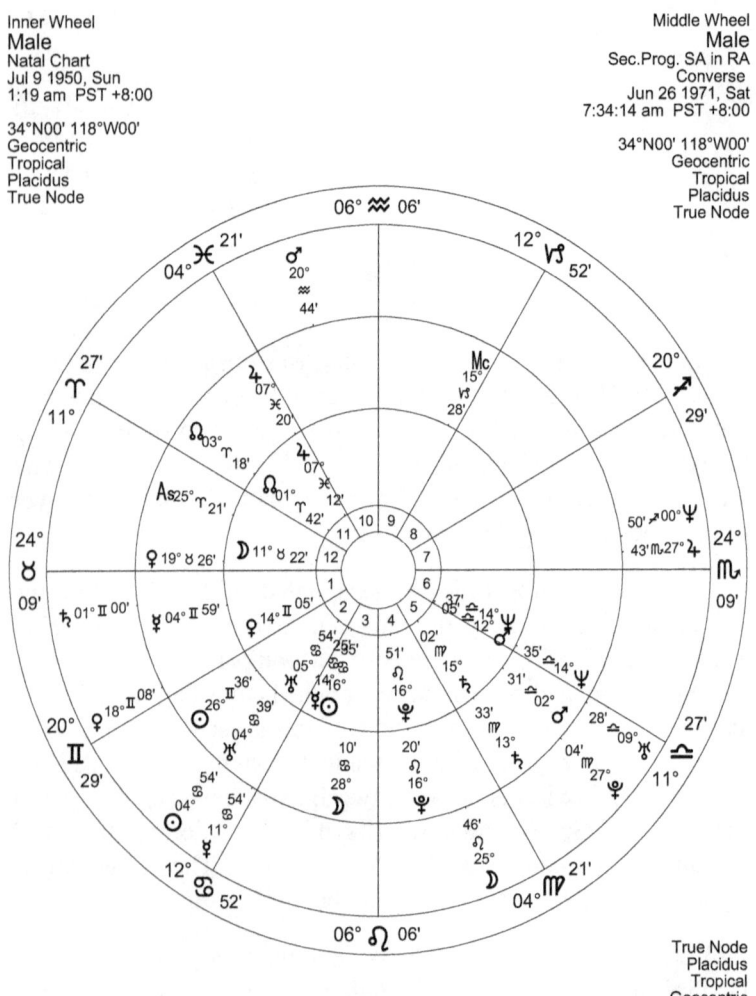

sure, square Venus, and quincunx Mars, Neptune, and the Point of Accident.

There are no planets in violent signs, none in critical degrees, and none at the degree of the lunar Nodes. The Sun, ruler of the fourth (end of life) is conjunct Mercury, ruler of the critical fifth cusp (recklessness), with both of them in the third of travel in close square to a Mars-Neptune conjunction in the sixth house of health, semisextile Pluto, and sextile Saturn.

Mars is in detriment, co-ruler of the seventh (other people and one's doctor), trine the rising Venus, and ruler of the twelfth of hospitals. Neptune rules the eleventh (events beyond our control).

The Moon in the twelfth, ruling the travel third, is in exaltation, conjunct Part of Catastrophe, opposition Part of Peril, quincunx Mars and Neptune, square Pluto, and sextile Sun and Mercury.

Pluto in Leo (sign of the heart) rules the seventh and is in the fourth, showing that the end of life would come through the activity of others. It is close to the midpoint of Venus, ruler of the Ascendant, and Neptune, ruler of the critical eleventh house, square Part of Peril, and at the midpoint of Sun/Mercury/Saturn.

There is a yod in this chart with Pluto receiving the sextile from the Mars-Neptune conjunction; both of them are quincunx (death angle) Jupiter, ruler of the eighth. The outlet, or point of manifestation, is Saturn in the pleasure fifth, which is at the midpoint of the Pluto/Mars/Neptune sextile.

Fixed Stars

These fixed-star conjunctions emphasize the Jupiter/Mars/Saturn influence of the yod:

- Venus conjunct Rigel (nature of Jupiter and Mars).
- Mars conjunct Algorah (nature of Mars and Saturn).
- Jupiter conjunct Skat (nature of Saturn and Jupiter).

Primary Directions
- Venus at 4 Cancer 40, square the Point of Danger, 21 minutes away from a conjunction to natal Uranus.
- Uranus at 26 Cancer 34, critical, cardinal sign.
- Mercury at 5 Leo 04, semisextile natal Uranus.
- Pluto at 7 Virgo 24, opposition natal Jupiter, ruler of the natal eighth, semisextile midpoint of Accidents, semisquare natal Part of Fatality.
- Saturn at 5 libra 43, square natal Uranus.
- Mars at 2 Scorpio 09, degree of natal Nodes for a loss.
- Neptune at 5 Scorpio 16, sextile natal Uranus.
- Jupiter at 27 Pisces 52, semisextile natal Moon, sesquisquare natal third cusp.
- Part of Fortune at 9 Aries 23, semisquare natal Ascendant.

Converse Directions
- Converse Ascendant at 3 Taurus 22, trine natal Part of Death, semisquare natal Fortuna, quincunx Point of Danger.
- Converse Uranus at 15 Gemini 21, square natal Saturn.
- Converse Pluto at 26 Cancer 16, critical, cardinal.
- Converse Mars at 20 Virgo 51, square natal eighth cusp.
- Converse Jupiter at 16 Aquarius 34, opposition natal Pluto.
- Converse Midheaven at 15 Capricorn 26, trine natal Saturn.
- Converse fourth cusp sextile natal Saturn.
- Converse Part of Fatality at 1 Cancer 51, semisquare natal Pluto.

Preceding Eclipses
- March 7, 1970, total solar eclipse at 16 Pisces 44, opposition natal Saturn, quincunx (death angle) natal Pluto, conjunct natal Fortuna, trine natal Part of Peril.
- August 17, 1970, partial lunar eclipse at 23 Aquarius 00, opposition natal Mercury, semisextile natal Part of Fatality,

square natal Ascendant.
- August 31, 1970, annular solar eclipse at 8 Virgo 04, opposition natal Jupiter, semisquare progressed Mars.
- February 25, 1971, partial solar eclipse at 6 Pisces 08, conjunct natal and progressed Jupiter, trine natal and progressed Uranus, quincunx natal IC.
- June 22, 1971 (four days before the event), partial solar eclipse at 28 Cancer 55, semisquare natal Venus and progressed Ascendant.

Tertiary Directions
- Tertiary Saturn, ruler of tertiary Ascendant, in tertiary eighth house.
- Tertiary Sun, in violent Aries in tertiary third and natal twelfth, quincunx tertiary Saturn.
- Tertiary Jupiter opposition tertiary Saturn.
- Tertiary Venus, ruler natal Ascendant, conjunct natal Ascendant, in tertiary fourth and ruling it, conjunct Caput Algol, sesquisquare natal Mars.
- Tertiary third and ninth cusps critical at 13 degrees cardinal, tertiary Ninth conjunct natal Neptune.
- Tertiary Moon at 29 degrees rules tertiary seventh, in Gemini sign of transportation, conjunct tertiary Part of Fatality also at 29 degrees in tertiary fifth.
- Tertiary Mars, ruler of tertiary third, conjunct Mercury in tertiary third, the latter ruling tertiary eighth.
- Tertiary Neptune in natal ninth, opposition tertiary Sun, quincunx natal Moon.
- Tertiary Ascendant trine natal Ascendant, agreeing with what the natal Ascendant promised at birth.
- Tertiary fourth cusp quincunx natal Neptune, sextile natal Mercury.
- Tertiary Fortuna, critical at 0 cardinal, semisquare natal Pluto.
- Tertiary Part of Peril conjunct tertiary eighth, conjunct na-

tal fifth cusp, sextile natal and tertiary Uranus.
- Tertiary Part of Death conjunct natal South Node.

Secondary Progressions
- Progressed Ascendant square natal Saturn.
- Progressed Mercury semisquare natal Mars, square natal Ascendant.
- Progressed Venus conjunct progressed Uranus, trine natal Jupiter, conjunct progressed fourth cusp.
- Progressed Sun sernisextile natal Uranus, quincunx progressed Jupiter, minutes from a conjunction to the Point of Accidents.
- Progressed Mars sesquisquare natal Jupiter, square natal Part of Fatality.
- Progressed Uranus trine natal Jupiter.
- Progressed fourth cusp semisquare natal Mars.
- Progressed Part of Peril square natal Jupiter, trine progressed Sun, quincunx progressed Venus and Uranus.
- Progressed Part of Fatality square natal Part of Catastrophe.
- Progressed Part of Death opposition natal Part of Fatality, quincunx natal Mercury.
- Progressed Part of Catastrophe at critical four degrees mutable, square natal fifth and eleventh cusps.
- Progressed Moon just past semisextile natal Jupiter, quincunx progressed Venus and Uranus.
- Progressed Fortuna at 18 Sagittarius 00, square natal Fortuna, sextile progressed Moon.
- Progressed Full Moon April 9, 1971, indicates the closing or the finishing of a cycle.

Transits
- Transiting Sun conjunct natal, progressed, and tertiary Uranus; conjunct progressed Venus, opposition natal Part of Death; square tertiary Part of Death and Fortuna; square

Point of Danger.
- Transiting Mercury semisquare natal Ascendant and progressed Mercury, quincunx progressed Moon, sextile tertiary Mercury, square tertiary Part of Catastrophe.
- Transiting Venus conjunct natal Venus and progressed Ascendant; sextile natal, progressed, and tertiary Pluto; quincunx natal Part of Peril; semisextile natal Sun; trine natal, progressed, and tertiary Neptune; square natal and progressed Saturn.
- Transiting South Node conjunct natal Pluto, square natal Part of Peril.
- Transiting Pluto conjunct tertiary Saturn, opposition tertiary Jupiter, sesquisquare natal Moon and Part of Catastrophe, square tertiary Moon and Part of Fatality.
- Transiting retrograde Uranus conjunct natal sixth cusp, sesquisquare natal Ascendant, quincunx natal Moon and Jupiter.
- Transiting retrograde Jupiter opposition natal Ascendant, semisquare natal Mars, sextile tertiary Saturn, trine tertiary Jupiter, semisextile tertiary Moon and Part of Fatality.
- Transiting retrograde Neptune semisquares natal and progressed Neptune, trine tertiary Fortuna, quincunx tertiary Mars.
- Transiting Mars square natal Ascendant; sextile natal eighth cusp and tertiary Sun; square tertiary Venus; opposition natal, progressed, and tertiary Pluto; quincunx natal Part of Fatality.
- Transiting Saturn sextile natal and progressed Uranus and Venus, semisquares natal Sun and Mercury, quincunx natal Part of Death.
- Transiting Moon semisquare natal and tertiary Uranus, trine tertiary Sun.

Chapter 6

Skid into Telephone Pole

Donna, a recent high school graduate, had experienced many health problems in her life that had at times limited her activities. Because of this, and also because of an inner compassion for others, she hoped to work with and help handicapped children. At the time of the accident she was working to earn money so she could later continue her studies and work toward her goal.

On September 21, 1971, at approximately 5:30 pm, 34N, she was driving home from work with her roommate as a passenger. She started down a freshly graveled hill and apparently the gravel caused the car to start sliding. She could not control the car and they skidded into a telephone pole. Donna was killed instantly of a broken neck and back (Leo on the Ascendant, Pluto in Leo in first house), while her roommate survived for three days, finally dying of massive head injuries.

In Donna's chart, Saturn is in violent Scorpio in the third hosue of travel, near the fourth house cusp, and square the Ascendant. (The event happened as she was going home.) Mercury and a detrimented Venus are also in violent Scorpio, square the first-house Pluto, ruler of the fourth. Both are in the fourth and so will have much to do with the end of her life, as will the Sun in the transportation sign of Sagittarius, also in the Fourth House, and square the Point of Accident in the first and trine Peril Jupiter in the eighth.

47

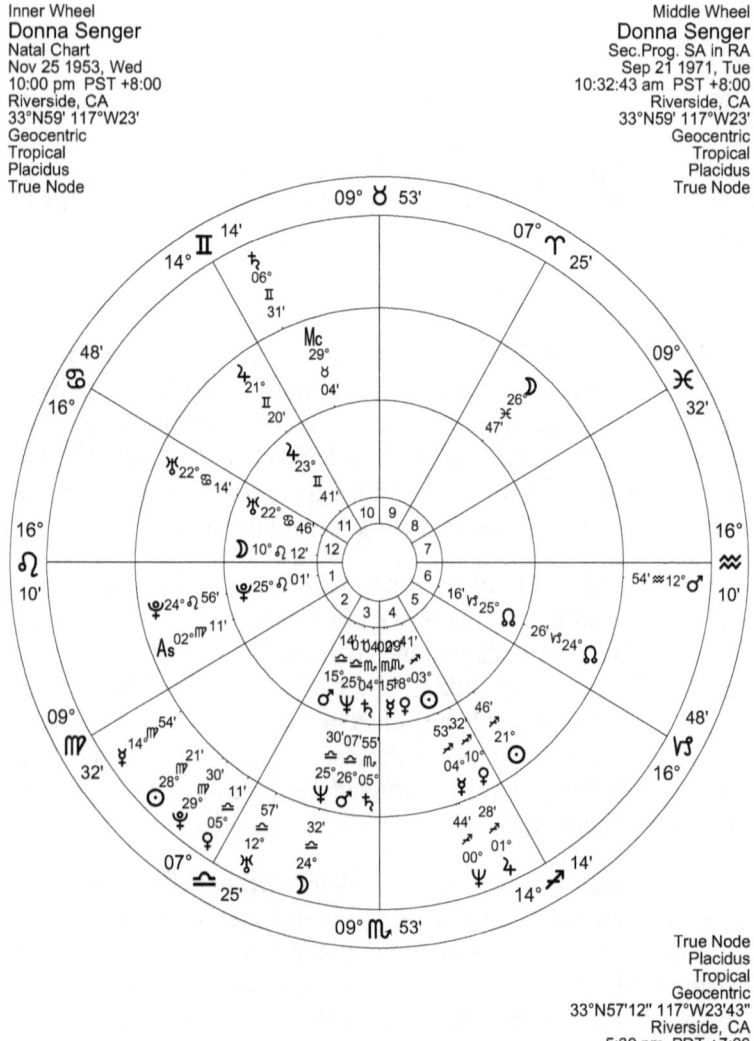

The ruler of the ninth and co-ruler of the fourth is a detrimented Mars in the travel third, exactly quincunx Part of Death in the eighth, conjunct the Point of Danger, and applying to a conjunction of Neptune, which rules the eighth house.

Jupiter is in the eleventh of friends and circumstances beyond one's control, and as co-ruler of the eighth house is also to be considered important in looking for potentials in this chart.

Jupiter is detrimented, retrograde, and elevated; it forms a wide opposition with the life-giving Sun. This is a rim opposition as the pattern of the chart is a bowl with Jupiter as the cutting planet.

The Part of Fortune is besieged by Mars and Saturn (hemmed in and threatened), while the public Moon is besieged by Uranus and Pluto. There are two Parts of Peril in this chart, as we have two rulers for the eighth cusp (Pisces). We see that danger on the road threatens from all sides (Mars near the third cusp, left side of the road, and Saturn near the fourth cusp, right side). The greatest danger came down the middle of the road because Neptune is conjunct the midpoint of danger in the middle of the third and fourth house cusps and conjunct the midpoint of danger in the middle of the third house.

The lunar Nodes are critical at 26 degrees cardinal, while the twelfth-house Moon is square Venus and Mercury and conjunct Peril Neptune.

Fixed Stars

The fixed stars show a strong Mercury-Mars-Saturn influence:

- Sun conjunct Graffia (nature of Mars and Saturn).
- Jupiter conjunct AI Hecka (nature of Mars).
- Mars conjunct Seginus (nature of Mercury and Saturn).
- Saturn conjunct Khamballa (nature of Mercury and Mars).
- Uranus conjunct Pollux, nature of Mars.

Preceding Eclipses
- February 10, 1971, total lunar eclipse at 21 Leo 00, critical degree, in natal first house (personal focus), conjunct natal and progressed Pluto and progressed Peril Neptune, sextile natal and progressed Jupiter, trine progressed Sun.
- February 25, 1971, partial solar eclipse at 6 Pisces 08, in natal seventh house close to natal eighth cusp, sesquisquare natal and progressed Uranus.
- July 22, 1971, partial solar eclipse at 28 Cancer 55, close to the natal South Node in the twelfth house.
- August 6, 1971, total lunar eclipse at 13 Aquarius 30, square natal Mercury and Venus in natal fourth (end of life), trine natal Mars in the third.
- August 20, 1971, partial solar eclipse at 27 Leo 15, in natal first house close to natal and progressed Pluto and progressed Peril Neptune.

Primary Directions
- Ascendant at 3 Virgo 49, square natal Sun, conjunct Point of Accident.
- Saturn at 21 Scorpio 33, critical degree, sesquisquare progressed Peril Jupiter.
- Venus at 5 Sagittarius 00, trine natal Part of Catastrophe.
- Uranus at 10 Leo 18, conjunct natal Moon.
- Peril Jupiter at 23 Aries 35, sextile natal Jupiter.
- Part of Death at 3 Aries 15, trine natal Sun, quincunx Point of Accident.
- Part of Fatality at 4 Leo 13, trine natal Saturn.

Converse Directions
- Converse Sun at 16 Scorpio 18, quincunx Part of Fatality.
- Converse Saturn at 16 libra 27, square natal Part of Fatality.
- Converse Uranus at 5 Cancer 12, square natal Part of Catastrophe.

- Converse Peril Neptune at 23 Cancer 44, semisextile natal Jupiter.
- Converse Part of Fatality at 29 Gemini 02, out of rope in travel sign.
- Converse IC at 22 libra 27 conjunct natal Fortuna.

Tertiary Directions

- Tertiary Ascendant opposition natal Mercury, quincunx Mars, sextile natal Part of Fatality.
- Tertiary Venus at same degree as tertiary lunar Nodes, ruler tertiary Ascendant, conjunct natal Mars.
- Tertiary Moon, ruler tertiary fourth, in tertiary fourth quincunx tertiary Mars in tertiary eighth house.
- Tertiary Midheaven at fatal 29 degrees.
- Tertiary Mercury, Sun, and Pluto conjunct tertiary fifth cusp, conjunct natal Pluto in natal first house.
- Tertiary Sun at same degree as natal lunar Nodes.
- Tertiary Jupiter in natal twelfth square natal and tertiary Neptune, square natal Fortuna.
- Tertiary Uranus in tertiary third conjunct tertiary Jupiter, square natal Neptune.
- Tertiary Saturn conjunct natal Saturn.
- Tertiary Neptune conjunct natal Neptune and Fortuna.
- Tertiary Part of Catastrophe at critical degree opposition tertiary Venus, square tertiary Nodes, conjunct natal Mars, semisquare tertiary Moon.
- Tertiary Part of Death semisquares natal Mars, sextile tertiary Part of Peril.
- Tertiary Fortuna conjunct natal seventh cusp, opposition natal Ascendant, and quincunx natal Part of Fatality.

Secondary Progressions

- Progressed Ascendant, changing signs (signals life changes), semisquare natal Mars.

- Progressed Mars completes conjunction to natal and progressed Neptune in the third house and at the degree of the progressed lunar Nodes (denoting a year of crisis).
- Progressed Sun completes its opposition to retrograde progressed Jupiter.
- Progressed Mercury, ruler of progressed Ascendant, conjunct natal Sun in the natal fourth, trine progressed Part of Fatality.
- Cusps of progressed fifth and eleventh houses are critical.
- Progressed Part of Fatality trine natal Sun.
- Progressed Part of Catastrophe opposition natal Fortuna, square natal and progressed Uranus.
- Progressed Moon moving from quincunx to natal Mars, conjunct natal Part of Death, trine natal Mercury, and now at 17 Pisces 00, a critical degree.
- Progressed Fortuna at 25 Scorpio 52 semisextile natal and progressed Neptune, ruler of natal eighth, semisextile progressed Mars, and square progressed Pluto, ruler of natal fourth (her luck had run out).

Transits

- Transiting Sun square Vertex, semisextile progressed Peril Neptune, sextile progressed IC, trine tertiary Moon, quincunx tertiary Mars, semisextile natal and tertiary Pluto, tertiary Sun, and Mercury.
- Transiting Jupiter and Neptune, conjunct, applying to conjunction of natal Sun and progressed Mercury, semisquare natal Mars, square progressed Ascendant, conjunct tertiary Part of Catastrophe, sextile tertiary Part of Peril.
- Transiting Mercury sextile natal Mercury and Venus, opposition progressed Moon and natal Part of Death.
- Transiting Venus sextile natal Sun and progressed Mercury, semisquare natal Venus, opposition natal Part of Catastrophe and progressed Part of Death, semisextile the Point of Accident.

- Transiting Mars and North Node trine natal Mars, semisextile tertiary Venus, in same degree as the tertiary Nodes.
- Transiting Saturn, stationary retrograde, sextile natal Peril Jupiter, quincunx progressed Saturn, opposition progressed Venus, semisquare progressed Part of Catastrophe.
- Transiting Uranus conjunct natal Mars, at same degree as tertiary lunar Nodes, conjunct tertiary Venus.
- Transiting Pluto at 29 degrees semisextiles progressed Peril Neptune, trine tertiary Moon, square tertiary Mars, sextile tertiary fourth cusp.
- Transiting Moon conjunct natal third cusp, opposition natal Part of Catastrophe and Peril Jupiter.

Chapter 7

Car Crash into Embankment

This man drove away from his home after an argument with his wife. Due to his upset condition he suffered a slight heart attack. Losing control of his car, he plowed head-on into an embankment on August 4, 1971 at 5:00 am, 34N.

Death occurred two days later of head injuries (Mars) and a crushed chest (Saturn and Sun in Gemini in the Fourth). There was a total lunar eclipse that day at 13 Aquarius 30, in the natal twelfth house (hospitals), close to his natal Ascendant, sesquisquare natal Moon, square tertiary Mars, and conjunct tertiary Uranus. Transiting Mercury had moved forward to 8 Virgo 00 to complete its conjunction to progressed Mercury, while transiting Venus moved to 9 Leo 08, completing its opposition to natal Uranus and to tertiary Moon, bringing to a close another life cycle.

In this chart we find Jupiter in the eleventh house of the far future in violent Capricorn, and Mars at a critical degree in violent Aries.

Mercury, fourth-house ruler, is besieged by Neptune and by critical Pluto, while Venus, ruler of the eighth house and the travel third, is besieged by Mars and Saturn. The Ascendant is besieged by Uranus and Mars.

Mars is the fulcrum of the cardinal T-cross with Jupiter in opposition to Neptune.

Venus is conjunct the third cusp from the second (twelfth house for the third) and square Uranus.

Uranus, ruling the Ascendant, is retrograde in the twelfth house, trine the fourth-house Saturn, its co-ruler.

The Sun in travel sign Gemini is with Saturn in the fourth house, square the Moon, and intercepted in the public seventh house.

The Moon is quincunx Mars and Part of Death, sextile Neptune, and trine Fortuna.

While the lunar Nodes are at 29 degrees, there are no planets at that degree so their influence is lessened or delayed. (His age at the event was 58 years, or twice 29.)

Mercury is quincunx Uranus and conjunct the critical Pluto, ruler of the travel ninth.

Fixed Stars
- Mars conjunct Vertex (nature of Mars and Moon).
- Venus conjunct Hamel (nature of Mars and Saturn).
- Part of Fortune conjunct Capulus (nature of Mars and Mercury).
- Saturn conjunct Aldeberan (nature of Mars).
- Sun conjunct Capella (nature of Mars and Mercury).
- Neptune conjunct Procyon (nature of Mercury and Mars).
- Moon conjunct Zavijava (nature of Mercury and Mars).

Preceding Eclipses
- February 10, 1971, total lunar eclipse at 21 Leo 00, critical degree, in natal seventh house, trine natal Fortuna, opposition natal Part of Death, sextile natal Sun.
- February 25, 1971, partial solar eclipse at 6 Pisces 08, in natal first house, square natal fourth cusp, square natal Saturn,

quincunx natal eighth cusp, semisextile natal Uranus and sextile progressed Jupiter.
- July 22, 1971, partial solar eclipse at 28 Cancer 55, conjunct progressed Neptune and fourth cusp, sesquisquare progressed Part of Peril, square natal Mars.

Primary Directions

- Ascendant at 14 Aries 15, square natal Part of Peril.
- Mars at 23 Gemini 44, semisextile natal Fortuna.
- Saturn at 6 Leo 32, sextile natal fourth cusp.
- Mercury at fatal 29 Leo 55, same degree as the natal Nodes.
- Moon at 24 Scorpio 07, trine natal Neptune.
- Fortuna at 20 Cancer 29, semisextile natal Sun.
- Part of Death at 23 Aries 27, semisextile natal Fortuna.
- Part of Fatality at 2 Aries 54, square natal Mercury, semisquare Point of Danger.
- Part of Catastrophe at 0 Sagittarius 53, quincunx natal Pluto, semisquare natal Jupiter.

Converse Directions

- Converse Ascendant at fatal 29 Aquarius 06, same degree as natal Nodes, semisquare natal Part of Peril.
- Converse Venus at 9 Pisces 53, square natal Saturn, sesquisquare natal Neptune.
- Converse Pluto at 2 Taurus 43, sextile natal Mercury.
- Converse Sun at 23 Aries 15, semisextile natal Fortuna (not a strong enough aspect to help him).
- Converse Mercury at 5 Taurus 17, semisquare natal Sun.
- Converse Moon at fatal 29 Cancer 29, same degree as natal lunar Nodes.
- Converse Uranus at 9 Sagittarius 53, opposition natal Saturn, sesquisquare natal Neptune.
- Converse fourth cusp at 8 Aries 41, sesquisquare natal Fortuna.

- Converse Part of Peril at 17 Scorpio 36, opposition Point of Danger.
- Converse Part of Catastrophe at 6 Leo 15, sextile natal fourth cusp.

Tertiary Directions
- Tertiary Venus, ruler of tertiary Ascendant in tertiary fourth, square tertiary Part of Peril, conjunct natal sixth cusp, quincunx tertiary Uranus.
- Jupiter, ruler of tertiary eighth house, retrograde in tertiary twelfth and void of course, opposition natal Moon and conjunct natal North Node.
- Moon, ruler of tertiary fourth house, conjunct natal Uranus, square natal Venus in opposition to the dignified tertiary Sun and tertiary Neptune; latter two planets conjunct in tertiary fourth, square natal Ascendant and Mars, square natal Venus, opposition tertiary Uranus, semisextile natal Pluto and Mercury.
- Tertiary Mars in tertiary first conjunct Part of Catastrophe and square tertiary Uranus, fulcrum of the fixed T-cross, trine natal Jupiter, in natal third house.
- Tertiary Mercury in tertiary third quincunx tertiary Uranus, sextile tertiary Mars, opposition natal Jupiter and Part of Peril.
- Tertiary Uranus sextile natal Jupiter, semisquare natal North Node.
- Tertiary Part of Catastrophe conjunct natal Point of Danger.
- Tertiary Part of Death trine natal Pluto, quincunx tertiary Sun and Neptune.
- Tertiary Part of Peril square natal Neptune.
- Tertiary Saturn semisextile natal Saturn.

Secondary Progressions
- Progressed Ascendant trine natal Jupiter and progressed Sun, semisquares natal and progressed Pluto.
- Progressed Mars sextile natal Mars, square natal Moon, trine natal Part of Death.
- Progressed Venus, critical degree, sextiles natal Saturn.
- Progressed Midheaven at same degree as natal Nodes.
- Progressed Sun trine natal Jupiter.
- Progressed Mercury trine progressed Jupiter, sesquisquare progressed Part of Death.
- Progressed Moon for July 1971 at 27 Sagittarius 43, moving away from conjunction of natal eleventh cusp and progressed Mars, from a square to natal Moon and a sextile to natal Part of Death and Mars, now semisextile progressed Neptune in natal third.
- Progressed Part of Fortune for July at 26 Leo 57, trine natal Mars, sextile progressed Mars, semisextile natal Moon.

Transits
- Transiting Sun in natal sixth hosue of health, in Leo (heart), conjunct progressed Venus, sextile natal Saturn, semisquare natal Moon, conjunct tertiary fifth cusp, square tertiary Mars, opposition tertiary Uranus.
- Transiting Venus opposition progressed Uranus and natal Part of Fatality, trine progressed Part of Fatality, conjunct tertiary Sun, opposition tertiary Moon, square tertiary Fortuna.
- Transiting Mercury quincunx natal Uranus, trine natal Venus, quincunx tertiary Moon.
- Transiting Pluto conjunct natal Moon, quincunx natal Mars and Part of Death, sextile progressed Neptune, square progressed Mars and Moon, semisextile progressed Fortuna, opposition tertiary Jupiter.
- Transiting Nodes at same degree as natal Part of Peril, tertiary Mercury, Mars, and Uranus.

- Transiting Jupiter, quincunx natal and progressed Mars, square natal Part of Death and progressed Fortuna, trine progressed Moon and tertiary Jupiter.
- Transiting Neptune, retrograde, quincunx natal and progressed Pluto, trine tertiary Neptune and Sun, square tertiary Part of Death.
- Transiting Mars at same degree as tertiary Nodes, sesquisquare natal Mercury, tertiary Pluto and natal Part of Catastrophe.
- Transiting Saturn, critical degree, conjunct natal fourth cusp, trine natal Part of Catastrophe, sextile progressed Part of Fatality, trine tertiary Ascendant, semisquare tertiary Venus.
- Transiting Moon at 15 Capricorn 34 conjunct natal Jupiter and Part of Peril, trine progressed Ascendant and Sun, trine tertiary Mars and Part of Catastrophe, semisextile natal Ascendant and tertiary Uranus.

Chapter 8

Car Collision

Hancock had been out of work for some time and drinking quite heavily. At 8:30 pm on January 3, 1967, he collided with another car at an intersection and was killed instantly (broken back, Neptune in Leo). The two people in the other car were injured, but both survived the event.

In this chart we find Venus, ruler of the third, and Mercury, ruler of the fourth, conjunct in the eleventh house, in violent Capricorn. Both are opposed by Pluto, ruler of the travel ninth and are square the Moon in violent Aries.

The Moon is in wide opposition to the eighth-house exalted Saturn; the latter is at the fatal 29 degrees. It rules the eleventh (far future) and is square the twelfth (self-undoing), which it also rules, thus carrying the light of its opposition to the Moon to the square of Mercury, Venus, and Pluto, forming a grand cardinal cross.

Mars in violent Scorpio is also in the eighth house, widely square retrograde Neptune in the sixth, and trine the rising Uranus.

The Sun is in opposition to Fortuna in the fourth house, while the dignified Jupiter is at home in its own ninth house at the degree of the Nodes, and square the Ascendant.

The Part of Peril and Part of Catastrophe are conjunct in the third of travel and square the Part of Death, which in turn is

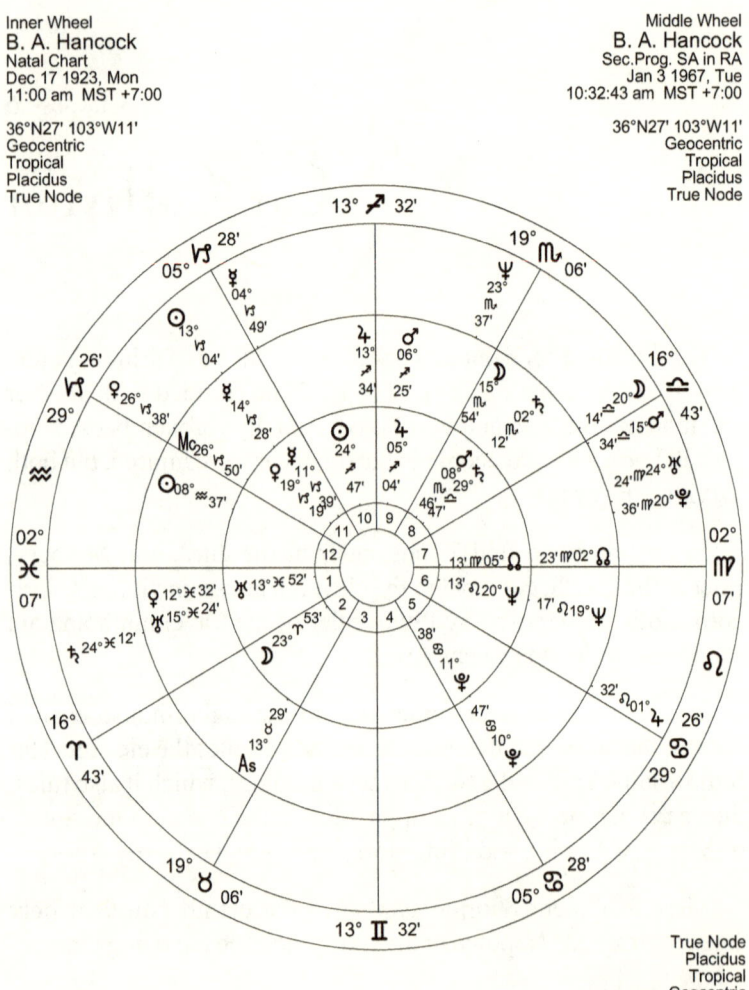

quincunx the twelfth house cusp, while Part of Fatality opposes Pluto.

Venus and Saturn are in mutual reception, giving him saving grace for many years. There are also two grand trines—one in fire and one in water.

Fixed Stars
- Neptune conjunct Algenubi (nature of Saturn and Mars).
- Sun conjunct Lesatch (nature of Mercury and Mars).
- Venus conjunct Deneb (nature of Mars and Jupiter).

Preceding Eclipses
- June 14, 1965, partial lunar eclipse at 22 Sagittarius 30, conjunct natal Sun, semisquare natal eighth house.
- November 23, 1965, annular solar eclipse at 0 Sagittarius 40, square natal Ascendant (personal focus), semisextile progressed Saturn.
- May 20, 1965, annular solar eclipse at 28 Taurus 56, in natal third house, square natal Part of Death.
- November 12, 1965, total solar eclipse at 19 Scorpio 45 (conjunct fixed star Serpentis, the cursed degree of the cursed sign), square natal and progressed Neptune, conjunct the natal ninth cusp.

Primary Directions
- Ascendant at 13 Aries 53, critical degree, trine natal Midheaven.
- Uranus at 26 Aries 18, critical degree.
- Mars at 20 Sagittarius 54, quincunx natal Part of Peril.
- Jupiter at 17 Capricorn 28, square natal Moon.
- The Sun at 6 Aquarius 40, semisextile natal Part of Fatality.
- Venus at 1 Pisces 08, conjunct natal Ascendant.
- Part of Death at 11 Libra 50, square natal Pluto.

- Part of Catastrophe at 3 Cancer 28, square Point of Danger.
- Midheaven at 25 Capricorn 26, quincunx natal Fortuna.

Converse Directions
- Converse Ascendant at 19 Capricorn 01, conjunct natal Venus.
- Converse Uranus at 1 Aquarius 26, semisextile natal Ascendant.
- Converse Moon at 5 Pisces 31, conjunct natal South Node, square natal Jupiter.
- Converse Pluto at 29 Taurus 21, conjunct the Pleiades (giving something to cry about), square natal Part of Death, quincunx natal Saturn, trine natal twelfth cusp (self-undoing).
- Converse Saturn at 17 Virgo 20, critical degree, quincunx natal Moon.
- Converse Sun at 11 Scorpio 48, trine natal Pluto.
- Converse Venus at 6 Sagittarius 16, semisextile natal Part of Fatality.
- Converse Part of Death at 16 Cancer 58, sesquisquare natal Ascendant.
- Converse Part of Catastrophe at 8 Aries 36, quincunx natal Mars.

Tertiary Directions
- Tertiary Ascendant conjunct fixed star Vindemiatrix, nature of Saturn and Mercury, semisextile natal Mars.
- Tertiary Mars conjunct tertiary eleventh cusp, square the tertiary eighth-house exalted Moon, semisextile natal Pluto.
- Tertiary Fortuna at same degree as tertiary and natal Nodes, trine natal Jupiter.
- Tertiary Saturn, ruler tertiary fourth, in natal eighth house, conjunct natal Mars, square tertiary Mars, Venus, Mercury,

and Neptune.
- Tertiary Moon conjunct natal Part of Peril and Part of Catastrophe, square tertiary Leo (spine) stellium, conjunct natal third cusp.
- Tertiary Venus, ruler of tertiary Ascendant and eighth house, conjunct Mars as part of a four-planet stellium, quincunx tertiary retrograde Jupiter in tertiary fourth.
- Tertiary Mercury quincunx tertiary Jupiter, quincunx natal Mercury.
- Tertiary Neptune critical at 21 degrees of fixed sign, trine natal Sun, square natal Part of Peril and Part of Catastrophe.
- Tertiary Pluto critical at 13 degrees cardinal, trine natal Uranus, opposition tertiary Jupiter.
- Tertiary eighth cusp at same degree as natal and tertiary Nodes, square tertiary Fortuna.
- Tertiary Part of Peril opposition tertiary Jupiter, sextile tertiary Moon.

Secondary Progressions
- Progressed Sun critical at nine degrees of a fixed sign.
- Progressed Venus conjunct natal Uranus, square progressed Jupiter, square natal Midheaven.
- Progressed Neptune, retrograde, conjunct the progressed fifth cusp (recklessness), opposition progressed Part of Fatality.
- Progressed Jupiter conjunct natal Mifheaven for years.
- Progressed twelfth cusp at 23 Pisces, degree of sorrow.
- Progressed Part of Catastrophe, at same degree as progressed Nodes, trine natal Point of Danger.
- Progressed Moon for January 1967, at 11 Scorpio 40, trine natal Pluto, semisextile progressed Part of Death.
- Progressed Fortuna for January at 8 Aquarius square natal Mars, minutes from conjunction to critical progressed Sun.

Transits
- Transiting Sun conjunct natal Mercury and Point of Accident; opposition natal, progressed, and tertiary Pluto; conjunct tertiary fourth cusp; square tertiary Ascendant; trine progressed Moon; sextile natal and progressed Uranus, square progressed Part of Death, quincunx tertiary Mars and eleventh cusp.
- Transiting Venus semisextile natal Sun; sesquisquare natal Mars; quincunx natal Part of Death, natal Fortuna, and tertiary Uranus; square natal Saturn; opposition tertiary Sun.
- Transiting Saturn in natal fifth house quincunx natal Saturn and natal Part of Death; square natal Fortuna; semisquare progressed Sun and Fortuna, sesquisquare natal Mars, progressed Moon, and tertiary Mars; conjunct tertiary Uranus; opposition tertiary Part of Death.
- Transiting Nodes at same degree as tertiary Pluto, progressed Venus, and natal Uranus.
- Transiting Jupiter, retrograde, square natal Point of Danger, sesquisquare progressed Uranus.
- Transiting Pluto and Uranus, both retrograde, square natal Sun, opposition tertiary Uranus, square natal Fortuna, trine natal Part of Peril and Part of Catastrophe, sextile tertiary Sun.
- Transiting Mars square natal Venus, opposition natal Moon, quincunx natal Part of Peril and Part of Catastrophe in tertiary fifth house, conjunct natal eighth cusp, quincunx natal and progressed Uranus and Venus, sextile tertiary Mercury, square tertiary Jupiter, sesquisquare natal Ascendant.
- Transiting Neptune in violent Scorpio in natal ninth, semisextile natal Sun, opposition natal Part of Peril and Part of Catastrophe, quincunx natal Fortuna, trine tertiary Uranus and Sun, sextile tertiary Part of Fatality.
- Transiting Mercury conjunct progressed ninth cusp, opposition progressed Part of Peril and Part of Fatality, sesqui-

square natal and progressed Neptune and progressed fifth cusp, sextile progressed Saturn, semisquare progressed Part of Fatality, square tertiary Ascendant in tertiary third house.

- Transiting Moon square natal Mercury and Pluto, conjunct progressed Part of Death, semisextile progressed Moon, quincunx natal Uranus and progressed Venus, trine progressed Sun and tertiary Part of Catastrophe, conjunct tertiary Ascendant, square tertiary Jupiter, sextile tertiary Mars, Venus, and Mercury.

Chapter 9

Accidental Electrocution

This young person was visiting relatives at latitude 34N when the event occurred at approximately 5:15 pm on December 2, 1969. He and a group of friends had decided to climb a power transmission pole, and he grasped a hot wire and was electrocuted. Death was instantaneous.

In the chart we find the Sun, ruler of the Leo Ascendant, in the eighth house, void of course, while the Ascendant is besieged by Uranus and Pluto.

Pluto, ruler of the fourth, rises in the map, conjunct the Point of Danger. It is opposition Venus and square Mars and Saturn, forming a fixed grand cross.

A detrimented Mars, co-ruling the fourth house, is in the tenth (high places) at the degree of the boy's age at the time of the event (fourteen), as is the Part of Death.

Retrograde Saturn, detrimented by house position, is in the fourth in violent Scorpio and rules the sixth of health.

Venus in the public Seventh is opposite the Point of Danger.

Neptune, ruler of the eighth, is in the travel third, retrograde and quincunx (death angle) the eighth house Sun. Jupiter, co-ruler of the eighth, is in the twelfth of self-undoing, and trine Saturn,

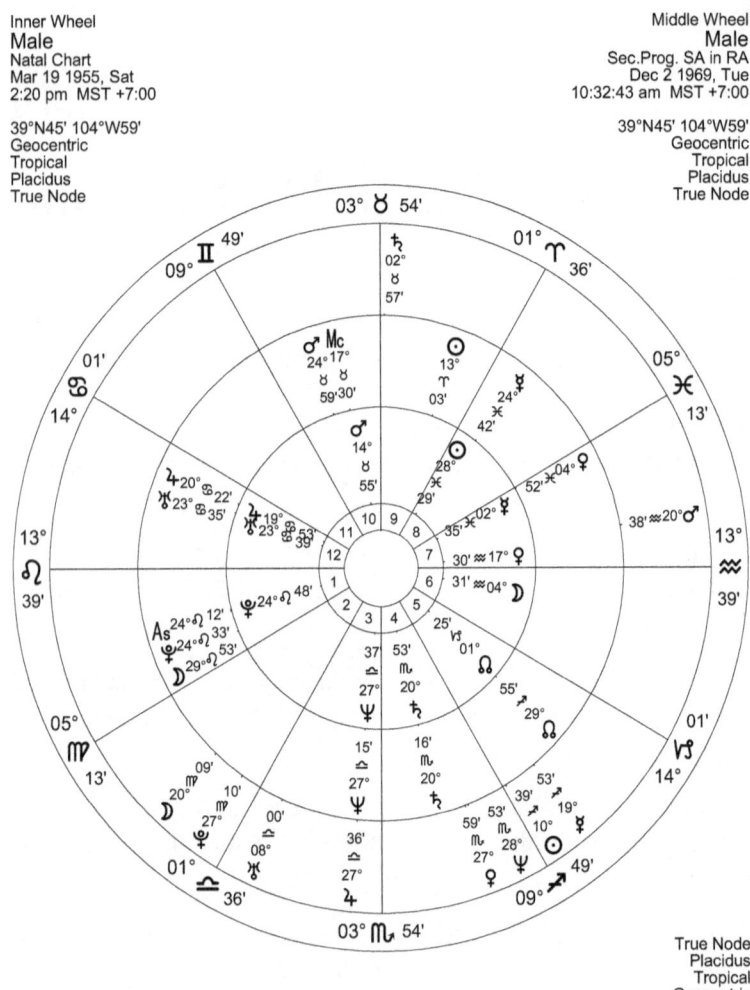

conjunct retrograde Uranus (electricity); both are square the third-house Neptune. Jupiter also rules the fifth house of recklessness and is besieged by Mars and Pluto, the two rulers of the fourth.

A detrimented Mercury close to the eighth cusp in the public seventh is sesquisquare Jupiter, trine the fourth cusp, and square Part of Catastrophe in the fourth.

Peril Jupiter is square Peril Neptune and trine the Point of Danger, which in turn is quincunx Peril Neptune.

The Moon in the sixth opposes the Ascendant.

Part of Death is square Fortuna, trine Mars, quincunx Venus, and trine Peril Neptune. It is also square the Point of Accident.

There is a yod comprised of the Pluto-Neptune sextile, both quincunx the eighth-house Sun, with the outlet, or point of manifestation, in Virgo.

The Moon and Uranus are in mutual reception; this saved him for fourteen years.

Fixed Stars

- Ascendant conjunct Acubens, nature of Saturn and Mercury.
- Neptune conjunct Markeb (nature of Saturn and Jupiter).
- Saturn conjunct Foramen (nature of Saturn and Jupiter).
- Moon conjunct Bos (nature of Saturn and Venus).
- Mercury conjunct Sadalmelik (nature of Saturn and Mercury).
- Sun conjunct Scheat (nature of Mars and Mercury).
- Mars conjunct Menkar (nature of Saturn).
- Uranus conjunct Pollux (nature of Mars).

Preceding Eclipses
- March 18, 1969, annular solar eclipse at 27 Pisces 16 conjunct natal Sun in natal eighth, quincunx natal and progressed Neptune, opposition progressed Part of Death.
- April 2, 1969, partial lunar eclipse at 12 Libra 53 in natal ninth house, conjunct progressed Sun and Peril Jupiter, sextile natal Mars, co-ruler natal and progressed fourth.
- August 27, 1969, partial lunar eclipse at 4 Pisces 06, critical degree, conjunct progressed Sun (ruler natal and progressed Ascendant), semisquare Peril Neptune and natal and progressed Jupiter.
- September 11, 1969, annular solar eclipse at 18 Virgo 48 trine progressed fourth cusp, semiextile Point of Danger, sextile natal and progressed Saturn in natal fourth.
- September 25, 1969, partial lunar eclipse at 2 Aries 27, conjunct natal ninth cusp, semisextile natal Mercury, sesquisquare progressed fourth cusp.

Primary Directions
- Ascendant at 28 Leo 20 quincunx natal Sun.
- Pluto at 9 Virgo 21 square natal Part of Catastrophe.
- Saturn at 5 Sagittarius 23, semisquare Peril Neptune.
- Moon at 19 Aquarius 17, quincunx natal Jupiter, trine Point of Accident.
- Venus at 2 Pisces 02, conjunct natal Mercury.
- Mercury at 17 Pisces 04, critical, semisextile natal Venus.
- Sun at 12 Aries 59, conjunct Peril Jupiter.
- Part of Death at 28 Virgo 56, opposition natal Sun.
- Mars at fatal 29 Taurus 27, conjunct the Pleiades (giving something to cry about).
- Jupiter at 4 Leo 24, opposition natal Moon.
- Part of Fatality at 20 Aries 44, quincunx Saturn, square Peril Neptune.

Converse Directions
- Ascendant at fatal 29 Cancer 22 semisquare natal Part of Death.
- Neptune at 13 libra 09, critical degree, sextile natal Ascendant.
- Saturn at 6 Scorpio 25 quincunx natal Part of Fatality.
- Moon at 20 Capricorn 19 conjunct Peril Neptune, quincunx natal Fortuna, sextile natal Saturn.
- Sun at 14 Pisces 01, opposition natal Part of Death, sextile natal Mars.
- Jupiter at 5 Virgo 25 sesquisquare Peril Neptune.
- Uranus at 9 Cancer 12, quincunx natal Part of Catastrophe.
- Fourth cusp at fatal 29 Libra 31, semisquare natal Part of Death.
- Part of Catastrophe at Scorpio 33, square natal Pluto.

Tertiary Directions
- Tertiary Ascendant in violent Capricorn opposition natal Uranus and tertiary Fortuna, semisquare natal Part of Catastrophe.
- Tertiary Uranus at the degree of natal Nodes, quincunx natal Mercury, opposition natal Venus, trine tertiary Moon.
- Tertiary Full Moon sesquisquare natal Pluto, opposition tertiary Venus, ruler of tertiary fourth in eighth house, trine natal Part of Catastrophe.
- Tertiary Mercury, ruler tertiary eighth house, conjunct tertiary and natal Neptune, sextile tertiary Pluto, trine tertiary Part of Fatality in first house.
- Tertiary Saturn still in violent Scorpio opposition natal Mars, quincunx natal Sun, rules tertiary Ascendant.
- Tertiary Jupiter conjunct tertiary Pluto, quincunx tertiary Ascendant, semisextile natal Uranus.
- Teritary Fortuna semisextile natal Pluto, square natal Neptune, quincunx tertiary Part of Peril and Part of Fatality.

- Tertiary Mars in tertiary eighth house square natal Fortuna, sextile natal Uranus and Saturn (at their midpoint), square tertiary Part of Peril, trine natal Peril Neptune.
- Tertiary fourth cusp square natal Venus.
- Tertiary Nodes at same degree as natal Fortuna, natal Saturn and Peril Neptune.
- Tertiary Part of Catastrophe opposition tertiary fourth cusp, square natal Venus.
- Tertiary sixth and twelfth cusps at critical degree.
- Tertiary Part of Death conjunct natal Fortuna, semisextile natal Uranus, opposition tertiary Part of Peril.
- Tertiary Part of Fatality at fatal 29 degrees.

Secondary Progressions
- Progressed Ascendant conjunct natal and progressed Pluto.
- Progressed Mars square natal and progressed Pluto, square progressed Ascendant.
- Progressed Venus, at critical degree, semisextile Peril Neptune, sesquisquare natal Jupiter, trine natal fourth cusp.
- Progressed Mercury at degree of sorrow, trine natal and progressed Uranus.
- Progressed Sun conjunct Peril Jupiter.
- Progressed eighth cusp at critical degree.
- Progressed Part of Catastrophe, conjunct progressed fifth cusp, square progressed Mercury.
- Progressed Part of Fatality square progressed Jupiter and Peril Neptune, quincunx natal and progressed Saturn.
- Peril Jupiter at critical degree.
- Progressed Jupiter completed trine to Saturn.

Transits
- Transiting Sun conjunct natal Part of Catastrophe and tertiary eleventh cusp of circumstances, trine tertiary Moon, sextile tertiary Sun, semisquare tertiary Ascendant.

- Transiting Venus conjunct transiting Neptune in violent Scorpio, trine natal Sun, semisextile natal Neptune and tertiary Mercury and Neptune.
- Transiting Mercury quincunx natal Jupiter, trine the Point of Danger, opposition Point of Accident, square tertiary Jupiter and Pluto, semisextile progressed fourth cusp, semisquare natal Moon.
- Transiting Moon quincunx natal and progressed Jupiter; square progressed and tertiary fourth cusps; conjunct natal Venus; opposition natal Pluto, Point of Danger, tertiary Jupiter; square natal and progressed Saturn and tertiary Part of Catastrophe; trine natal Fortuna; semisextile Peril Neptune.
- Transiting Saturn, retrograde, conjunct natal Midheaven, square natal Moon and progressed Peril Neptune, sextile progressed Venus, semisquare Point of Accident, square tertiary Uranus.
- Transiting Pluto opposition natal Sun, conjunct progressed Part of Death, semisextile natal and progressed Neptune and tertiary Mercury and Neptune, quincunx tertiary Part of Peril, semisextile tertiary Pluto.
- Transiting Uranus sextile natal Ascendant and Part of Catastrophe, semisquare natal and progressed Pluto, opposition natal Part of Fatality and tertiary Moon, conjunct tertiary Sun.
- Transiting Jupiter conjunct natal and progressed Neptune and tertiary Mercury and Neptune, quincunx natal Sun, trine tertiary Part of Fatality, sextile tertiary Pluto.

Chapter 10

Hit by Truck

On 19 March 1973, at 4:13 pm, this young newlywed man was on his way home from work, riding his motorcycle. He was stopped for traffic when the brakes of a semi-truck failed and the truck hit him. Death was instantaneous.

This young man's chart has violent Capricorn on the Ascendant at a critical degree, with a critical Uranus, retrograde, exactly opposing it from the seventh house of open enemies.

Saturn, the chart ruler, is critical at four degrees mutable, at the degree of the lunar Nodes (6 X 4 = 24, his age at the event), widely square Mars, in the eighth, along with Pluto, ruler of the eleventh of circumstances. The eighth cusp is also at the degree of the Nodes in square aspect to them.

In the ninth house (travel) we find Venus, strong in its own sign, conjunct Neptune, ruler of the third of travel, besieged by Saturn and Neptune.

The eleventh-house Sun, ruler of the eighth and fulcrum of a fixed T-cross, is in violent Scorpio, square the Moon and Pluto and semi-sextiling the twelfth-house Mars, ruler of the fourth.

In the third house we find Part of Peril waiting by the side of the road in quincunx aspect to Venus, and quincunx Venus and Neptune, square Mars and trine the Sun. The Part of Misfortune

77

Inner Wheel
Male
Natal Chart
Nov 8 1948, Mon
10:00 am EST +5:00

26°N00' 080°W00'
Geocentric
Tropical
Placidus
True Node

Middle Wheel
Male
Sec.Prog. SA in RA
Mar 19 1973, Mon
10:32:43 am EST +5:00

26°N00' 080°W00'
Geocentric
Tropical
Placidus
True Node

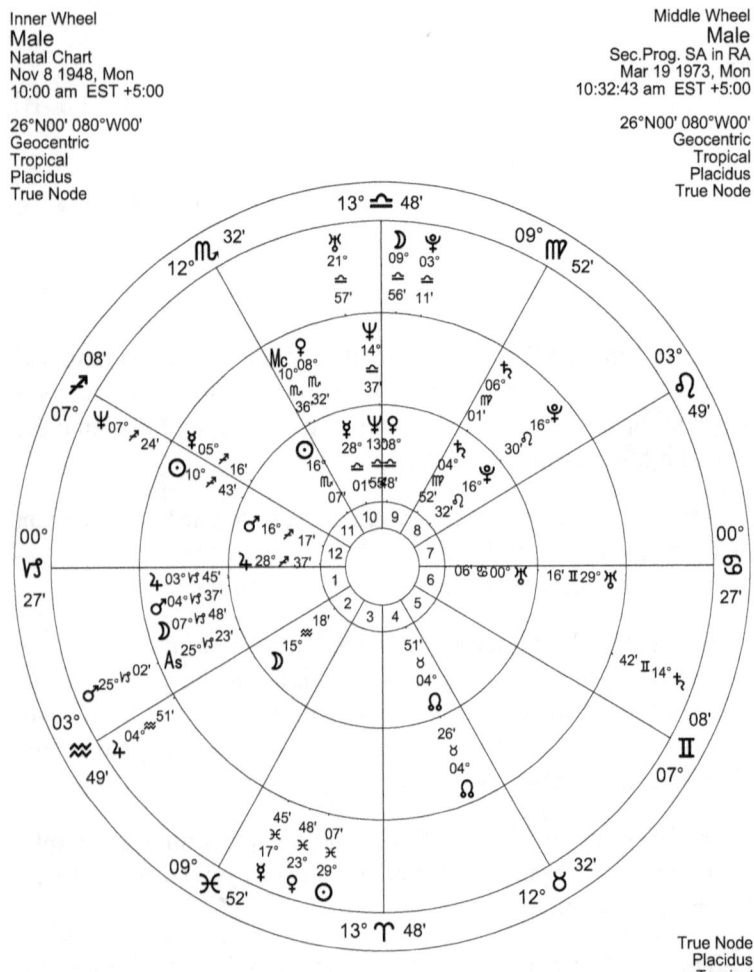

True Node
Placidus
Tropical
Geocentric
26°N00' 080°W00'

4:13 pm EST +5:00
Mar 19 1973, Mon
Event Chart
Transits Mar 19 1973
Outer Wheel

(Fortuna in Pisces) is in the third at 29 degrees (out of rope at birth), opposed by the Point of Accident in the ninth of travel.

Mercury, ruler of his house of health and work, makes only one aspect: a sextile to the twelfth house Jupiter, after which it enters void of course.

Part of Catastrophe in the eighth is square the Sun in violent Scorpio. The Sun rules the eighth, and is square the Point of Accident, quincunx Part of Death, and sesquisquare Uranus.

The Moon, ruling the seventh, is semisquare the Ascendant, opposition the eighth-house Pluto, and sesquisquare Uranus.

Neptune, critical at 13 degrees cardinal, is trine the Moon, sextile Mars and Part of Death, and opposition the fourth cusp.

Part of Death in the sixth is trine Part of Fatality and semisquare the eighth-house cusp and the North Node.

Fixed Stars

- Venus conjunct Vindemiatrix (nature of Saturn and Mercury).
- Neptune conjunct Algorab (nature of Mars and Saturn).
- Mercury conjunct Markeb (nature of Saturn and Jupiter).
- Mars conjunct Sabik (nature of Saturn and Venus).
- Jupiter conjunct Sinistra and Spiculum (nature of Saturn and Venus).
- Part of Fortune conjunct Scheat (nature of Mars and Mercury).

Preceding Eclipses

- January 30, 1972, total solar eclipse at 9 Leo 00 in natal eighth house, semisquare Point of Accident and opposition the Moon.
- January 16, 1972, total solar eclipse at 25 Capricorn 25 in natal first house, square Mercury, sextile Fortuna, trine

Point of Accident.
- July 10, 1972, total solar eclipse at 18 Cancer 37 square Neptune, trine natal Sun and quincunx natal Mars.
- July 26, 1972, partial lunar eclipse at 2 Aquarius 00, in ra~ First House, opposition natal Eighth Cusp, quincunx Saturn.
- January 4, 1973, partial solar eclipse at 14 Capricorn 08 in natal first, square Neptune, semisextile the Moon, quincunxe the eighth-house Part of Catastrophe and Pluto, sextile the Sun, quincunx Part of Death, square the fourth cusp.

Primary Directions
- Saturn at 28 Virgo 54 square natal Jupiter.
- Sun at 10 Sagittarius 08 semisquare the Point of Danger.
- Part of Fatality at 13 Scorpio 23 semisextile natal Neptune, semisquare natal Jupiter.
- Part of Catastrophe at 8 Virgo 36 semisextile natal Venus.
- Part of Death at 13 Cancer 18, critical degree, square natal Neptune.

Converse Directions
- Converse Saturn at 10 Leo 52 quincunx natal third cusp.
- Converse Neptune at 19 Virgo 55 semisquare natal South Node, square natal Part of Death, semisextile natal Part of Fatality.
- Converse Mercury at 4 libra 02 at same degree as natal Nodes, semisextile natal Saturn, sextile natal eighth cusp.
- Converse Jupiter at 4 Sagittarius 35, critical degree, at same degree as Nodes, square natal Saturn.

Tertiary Directions
- Violent Scorpio rises sextile to natal Point of Accident, with its two rulers Pluto and Mars, conjunct in the tertiary

ninth house, both conjunct natal Pluto; it is quincunx tertiary Jupiter, opposition natal Moon, square tertiary Venus in violent Scorpio.
- Tertiary Pluto at same degree as tertiary Nodes square tertiary Part of Death, trine natal Mars, square natal Sun, opposition tertiary Fortuna.
- Tertiary Mars square natal Sun, tertiary Venus and Part of Death; opposition tertiary Fortuna; sesquisquare tertiary Moon.
- Tertiary Uranus, ruler tertiary fourth house, in tertiary eighth at same degree as the natal Nodes, sextile natal Saturn, semisextile natal eighth cusp, square tertiary Sun.
- Tertiary Fortuna, in tertiary third house, conjunct natal Moon, square natal Venus and Part of Death, semisquare natal Fortuna and tertiary Moon.
- Tertiary Moon conjunct natal Jupiter, square natal Fortuna, semisextile tertiary fourth cusp, sextile natal Mercury.
- Tertiary Mercury, ruler tertiary fourth; conjunct natal and tertiary Neptune, tertiary South Node, and natal Midheaven; opposition natal fourth cusp; trine tertiary Fortuna and natal Moon.
- Tertiary Saturn conjunct natal ninth cusp, square natal Mars, semisquare natal Mercury.
- Tertiary Part of Catastrophe sextile tertiary eighth cusp, quincunx tertiary Jupiter exactly, on natal eighth cusp.
- Tertiary Part of Fatality sextile natal Ascendant and Uranus, trine tertiary Uranus, sextile natal Saturn.
- Tertiary Sun semisquare tertiary Ascendant, conjunct natal Venus.
- Tertiary fifth and eleventh cusps critical, square natal Ascendant.
- Tertiary Jupiter in violent Capricorn in natal first house, conjunct tertiary third cusp, square natal Mercury and natal Point of Danger.

Secondary Progressions
- Progressed Ascendant trine Point of Accident, sesquisquare progressed Part of Catastrophe.
- Progressed Mercury, now ruling progressed eighth, at critical degree, conjunct critical progressed eleventh cusp, at same degree as natal Nodes, sextile progressed Mars, square natal Saturn, semisquare natal Part of Fatality.
- Progressed Sun semisquare the Point of Danger.
- Progressed Venus semisextile natal Venus and progressed Part of Catastrophe.
- Progressed Mars trine natal Saturn, at same degree as natal Nodes.
- Progressed eighth cusp trine natal Ascendant, sextile natal Uranus and seventh cusp.
- Progressed Midheaven at critical degree.
- Progressed twelfth cusp conjunct natal Jupiter.
- Progressed Moon just past conjunction of progressed Mars, sextile progressed Mercury, trine natal Saturn, square to progressed Part of Peril.

Transits
- Transiting Sun at fatal 29 degrees conjuncts natal Fortuna; square natal Jupiter, progressed Uranus, and tertiary Moon; sesquisquare natal Part of Catastrophe; semisquare natal Moon and tertiary Fortuna; semisextile tertiary fourth cusp.
- Transiting Venus at degree of sorrow opposition natal Point of Accident, trine tertiary Ascendant.
- Transiting Mercury, retrograde, at critical degree, quincunx natal North Node and Pluto, at same degree as tertiary Nodes, quincunx tertiary Pluto, sextile tertiary Part of Death, trine tertiary Venus, square natal Mars. (Sun, Venus, and Mercury are in natal third house.)
- Transiting Saturn in travel Gemini trine natal, progressed, and tertiary Neptune and natal Midheaven; opposition natal Mars; quincunx natal Sun and tertiary Venus; sextile natal

fourth cusp, Part of Catastrophe, and natal, progressed, and tertiary Pluto and tertiary Mars; in the tertiary first house.
- Transiting Nodes critical at same degree as natal Neptune, conjunct progressed Part of Death.
- Transiting Pluto, retrograde, in natal ninth house, square progressed Jupiter, conjunct tertiary Sun and eleventh cusp, square natal Ascendant.
- Transiting Uranus, retrograde, conjunct Point of Danger, square tertiary Jupiter.
- Transiting Mars in natal first house square Point of Danger, semisquare progressed Sun, conjunct tertiary third cusp.
- Transiting Jupiter at degree of natal Nodes, quincunx natal Saturn and tertiary Uranus, sesquisquare natal Part of Death, trine progressed fifth cusp, conjunct natal second cusp, opposition natal eighth cusp, semisextile progressed Mars, sextile progressed Part of Peril.
- Transiting Moon trine natal Part of Death, semisquare natal Saturn, progressed Mercury, and eleventh cusp.

Chapter 11

Death by Fall

The accident occurred April 9, 1972, at approximately 9:15 pm. This young man was planning to become an electrical engineer and was working for a power company. He was trying to race his two coworkers down a portable ladder for electric poles when he slipped and fell. He landed on some sandbags then bounced to the ground. Death was instantaneous.

Iincluded here is the marriage chart, as it is very pertinent to the event. Our young man had been married only two months minus one day when the accident occurred.

In a marriage chart the Ascendant always represents the husband, while the wife is represented by the ruler of the Descendant. Thus, Mercury, ruler of the Ascendant, is conjunct Jupiter, ruler of the seventh, along with Venus, the North Node, and Fortuna, all in violent Capricorn in the eighth house.

Mercury is quincunx the public Moon, ruler of his third house, and the fourth cusp (his end of life).

The zero degree Sun, also representative of the male partner, is in his ninth house, semisextile Part of Catastrophe. The solstice point is at the fatal 29 degrees of violent Scorpio.

Retrograde Saturn, ruler of his eighth, is trine Part of Death and quincunx the Point of Accident, It is opposition Mars with which it

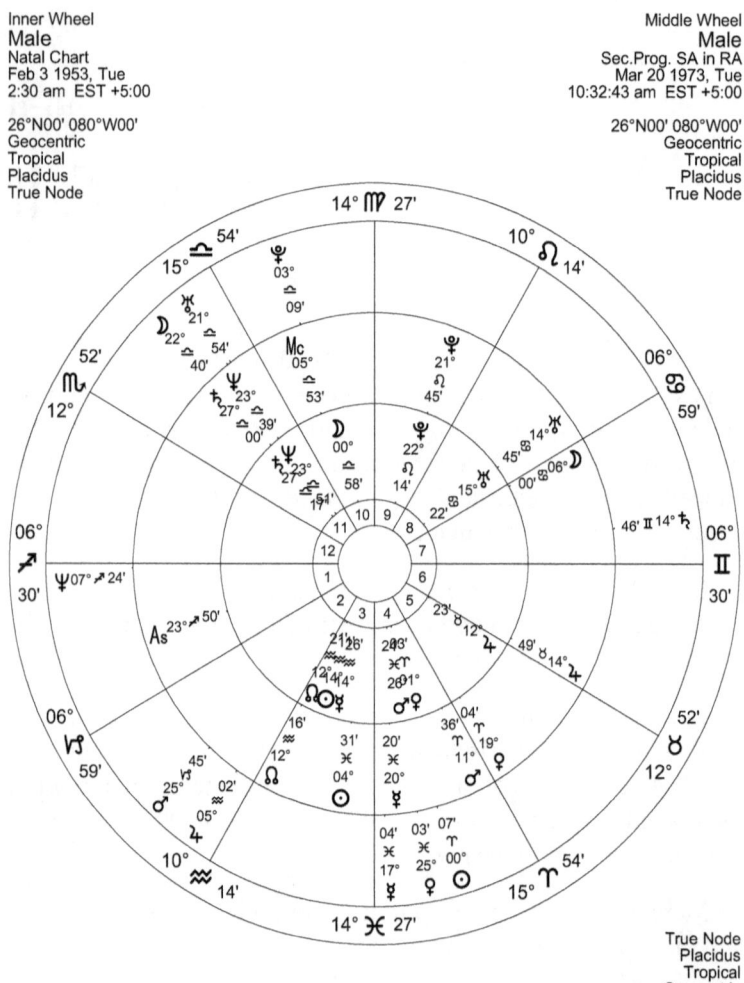

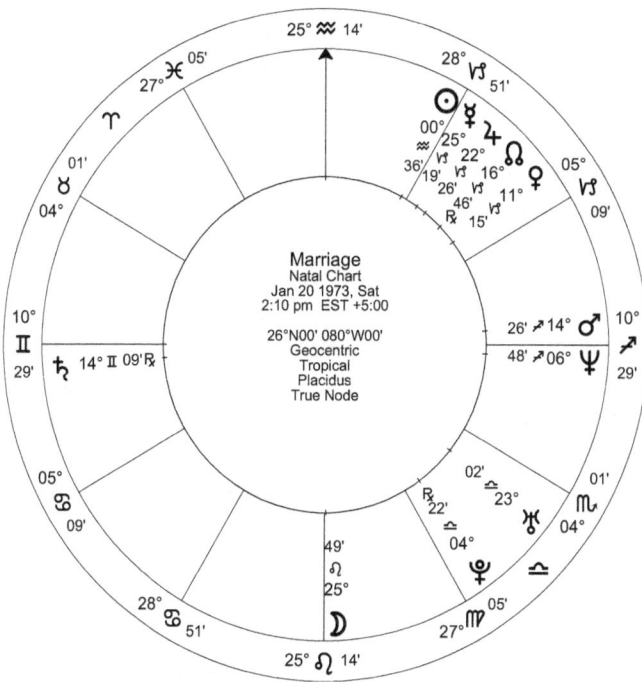

forms a mutable T-cross with the Part of Danger as the fulcrum. Saturn rises in transportation Gemini with its Part of Peril sitting on the Ascendant (his physical body). The Ascendant and the Part of Peril are quincunx (death angle) Venus, the lesser benefic, and the Point of Accident.

The Moon, ruler of his third, is exactly conjunct the fourth cusp and quincunx the eighth-house Mercury.

The Part of Fortune sits on the eighth cusp square Pluto, ruler of his sixth of health and her twelfth of sorrow, in quincunx aspect to the Ascendant and the Part of Widowhood.

Pluto is trine the Part of Widowhood and the Sun and quincunx Part of Catastrophe. Neptune, the planet of widowhood in travel sign Sagittarius, opposes the Part of Widowhood, the Ascendant and the Part of Peril from the sixth house (her twelfth of sorrows).

It is semisquare Uranus and its dispositor, the eighth-house Jupiter, while Jupiter is square Part of Fatality and Uranus.

Transits
- By March 20 the Moon had moved only one degree, which moved Fortuna to a sextile with the sixth-house (work) Neptune. By transit, Mars was conjunct natal Mercury, quincunx natal Moon and fourth cusp, and sesquisquare natal Part of Peril.
- Transiting Mercury was retrograde at a critical degree trine the Part of Accident, while transiting Venus was sextile natal Jupiter and Mercury, and quincunx natal Uranus and Part of Fatality.
- Transiting Sun at the fatal 29 degrees was trine the solstice point of the natal Sun.
- Transiting Saturn, direct, was conjunct natal Saturn, setting off what it promised in the natal chart.
- Transiting Uranus had retrograded one degree to complete its semisquare to natal Neptune, while transiting Neptune retrograde, had previously moved forward to complete the semisquare to natal Uranus.
- The transiting nodes, still in the natal eighth, were at a critical degree.
- Transiting Jupiter, in the natal ninth house, was trine natal Pluto.
- Transiting Pluto had retrograded one degree to complete its semisquare to the Part of Accident.

Thus did the marriage chart confirm the potential for a violent ending to the life as shown in the natal chart.

In the natal chart we find only Venus in a violent sign. It rules the sixth of work and co-workers and the eleventh of circumstances. It is detrimented, in the fourth (end of life), trine the Ascendant, and opposed by the critical Moon, ruler of the eighth. The latter is in the tenth house (high places), and both are square the retrograde eighth-house Uranus, ruler of the third, which in turn is square the Neptune-Saturn conjunction in the eleventh house.

There is a yod that is comprised of the Neptune-Saturn conjunction in sextile to the ninth-house Pluto, and all of them are quincunx the fourth-house Mars.

Pluto and Mars rule the twelfth of self-undoing, while Neptune rules the fourth with Jupiter as co-ruler. We find Jupiter straddling the cusp of the sixth house of work; it also rules the Ascendant, is in the same degree as the Nodes, and semisquare Mars. Jupiter is also square the Sun-Mercury combust aspect in the third house and retrograde Pluto and Part of Fatality in the ninth hosue, forming a fixed cross.

Part of Peril is in the eleventh in violent Scorpio, opposition Jupiter and Part of Catastrophe, square Sun and Mercury, and sesquisquare Mars.

Part of Death in the ninth is sextile Uranus, trine Jupiter, and quincunx Sun and Mercury.

The Ascendant is square Part of Death, quincunx Part of Catastrophe, semisextile Part of Peril, and quincunx the eighth cusp.

Sun and Mercury oppose the Part of Fatality and are besieged by Saturn and Mars. The third and ninth cusps are critical.

Fixed Stars
- Jupiter conjunct Menkar (nature of Saturn).
- Venus conjunct Difda (nature of Saturn).
- Neptune conjunct Arcturus (nature of Mars and Jupiter).
- Part of Fortune conjunct Pollux (nature of Mars).

Primary Directions
- Mars at 15 Aries 19 square natal Uranus.
- Jupiter at 1 Gemini 19, sextile natal Venus.

- Pluto at 11 Virgo 10 conjunct natal Part of Death.
- Moon at 19 Libra 54 sextile natal Part of Fatality.
- Neptune at 12 Scorpio 47 at degree of Nodes, opposition natal Jupiter.
- Part of Fortune at 11 Leo 52, sesquisquare natal Mars.
- Part of Catastrophe at 26 Taurus 15, sextile natal Mars.
- Part of Death at 00 Libra 41 conjunct natal Moon.

Converse Directions
- Converse Sun at 25 Capricorn 16 semisextile natal Ascendant.
- Converse Mars at 7 Pisces 29 sesquisquare natal Fortuna.
- Converse Venus at 12 Pisces 11 at same degree as Nodes, sextile natal Jupiter.
- Converse Jupiter at 23 Aries 29 opposition natal Neptune.
- Converse Uranus at 26 Gemini 27 square natal Mars.
- Converse Moon at 12 Virgo 04 at same degree as Nodes, trine natal Jupiter.
- Converse Neptune at 4 libra 57 semisquare natal Part of Fatality.
- Converse Saturn at 8 Libra 23 conjunct fixed star Vindemiatrix of the nature of Saturn and Mercury.
- Converse Fortuna at 4 Cancer 08 semisquare natal Part of Fatality.
- Converse Part of Fatality at 0 Leo 21 sextile natal Moon.

Tertiary Directions
- Tertiary Ascendant quincunx natal Venus, square tertiary Midheaven.
- Tertiary fourth cusp trine natal Venus, sextile natal Moon.
- Tertiary Venus conjunct tertiary second cusp, opposition tertiary eighth cusp, at same degree as tertiary Nodes, semisextile natal Saturn.
- Tertiary Saturn at fatal 29 degrees conjunct tertiary third

cusp, quincunx natal solstice point of natal Moon, opposition tertiary Peril Jupiter conjunct tertiary ninth cusp.
- Tertiary Sun conjunct natal and tertiary Neptune, quincunx tertiary Uranus.
- Tertiary Mercury, ruler of tertiary Ascendant, in violent Scorpio in tertiary third, square natal Sun and Mercury, opposition natal Jupiter, square natal and tertiary Pluto and tertiary Peril Neptune.
- Tertiary Jupiter, ruling tertiary fourth and co-ruling tertiary eighth, retrograde in tertiary tenth of high places, trine natal and tertiary Saturn.
- Tertiary Mars square tertiary Jupiter, opposition natal Mars.
- Tertiary Moon in sixth of health and work quincunx natal Part of Death, conjunct natal third cusp and natal Sun and Mercury, semisquare natal Mars.
- Tertiary Part of Fortune in tertiary fourth house trine natal Part of Fatality.

Secondary Progressions
- Progressed Ascendant sextile natal and progressed Neptune.
- Progressed Venus semisquare progressed Sun, semisextile progressed Mercury.
- Progressed Part of Death conjunct natal Moon.
- Progressed sixth cusp conjunct the Pleiades at 29 Taurus, giving something to cry about.
- Progressed Moon for April 1972 at 13 Gemini 48 sesquisquare natal, progressed, and tertiary Saturn; trine natal Sun and Mercury.
- Progressed Part of Fortune for April at 3 Aries 51 semisextile progressed Sun.

Transits
- Transiting Sun trine natal Part of Fatality and tertiary Fortuna, conjunct progressed Venus, semisextile pro-

gressed Mercury, semisquare progressed Sun, in tertiary eighth house, opposition tertiary Part of Death.
- Transiting Saturn conjunct tertiary Midheaven, square progressed Sun and tertiary Ascendant, opposition natal Ascendant, semisquare natal Fortuna, sextile natal fourth cusp.
- Transiting Mars opposition natal Ascendant, trine natal Part of Death, progressed Part of Fatality, and tertiary Moon; semisquare natal Fortuna and tertiary Uranus; quincunx natal Part of Peril; sesquisquare tertiary Sun and Neptune.
- Transiting Pluto, retrograde, conjunct natal Moon, opposition natal Venus and progressed Fortuna, quincunx progressed Sun.
- Transiting Uranus, retrograde, conjunct natal eleventh cusp, trine natal Sun and Mercury, quincunx progressed Mercury and Jupiter, opposition progressed Venus, square natal and progressed Uranus, semisextile tertiary Mercury, semisquare tertiary fourth cusp.
- Transiting Neptune retrograde and critical square tertiary Ascendant, in tertiary fourth house.
- Transiting Jupiter conjunct natal second cusp opposition natal eighth cusp; trine natal Part of Catastrophe, Jupiter, progressed Part of Fatality, natal Part of Death, tertiary Part of Fatality; square natal Midheaven.
- Transiting retrograde Mercury conjunct progressed Fortuna and fourth cusp in tertiary eighth, semisextile progressed Sun, quincunxc tertiary Ascendant, sesquisquare natal Part of Fatality.
- Transiting Nodes at same degree as natal Venus, tertiary Midheaven, and tertiary Part of Catastrophe.
- Transiting Moon at 27 Aquarius conjunct tertiary fourth cusp; trine natal, progressed, and tertiary Saturn; semisextile natal Mars, tertiary eighth cusp, and tertiary Peril Jupiter; quincunx tertiary Venus.

Summary

It usually has been said that accidental events—especially travel accidents—come primarily through the mutable signs. Yet the preceding examples show that the mutable T-crosses are minimally represented as there is only one in the group of natal charts. Other data show the same emphasis.

We find five cardinal crosses, one of which is a grand square, and five fixed; one is also a grand square. There are many yods, with some of the charts having more than one. Some have void-of-course planets, and there is a strong influence from the fixed stars in all of the charts.

Three charts have no T-squares at all, but they do have strong opposition and square aspects, and two of them have the Yod.

In the tertiary directions we find five mutable, three cardinal, and three fixed crosses, but we must remember that these are a form of progression, backing up or confirming other progressions, for development of the potential promised in the natal charts.

When looking for accident potentials in any chart we must remember that finding one or two of the items listed in the introduction, as well as any type of T-square, does not necessarily mean a fatal accident. It may not mean an accident at all.

As you reread the text and work with the charts, you will see how strong the potential was at birth. The interplay and involvement of all the progressions and the transits is also very strong. We must remember that the transiting planets are always making some sort of aspect to all the charts in the world, but they do not trigger accidents for everyone. Only those having the progressions activating the natal potential will be brought to fulfillment.

Part II
Potential Fulfilled: What Saved Them

Chapter 12

Drove into Drainage Ditch

On the morning of April 30, 1967, at approximately 7:10 am, Judy, a petite blue-eyed bride of three months (sister to Donna Senger, discussed in chapter 6), was driving to work, her view obscured by heavy fog.

Inability to see the road caused her to hit the dirt embankment of a drainage canal. Losing control of her car, she drove headlong into the canal which, luckily for her, was empty of water.

She sustained broken ribs and a deep cut on her leg. The more serious injuries were facial: her nose was badly smashed, and it was rebuilt with a plastic bridge insertion. She also has a plate in the center of her forehead. The scarring is remarkably minor for the extent of damage. Judy also had therapy for six years after the event for neck and back curvature that was caused by the impact of the car with the bottom of the ditch.

In Judy's chart there are no planets in violent signs, none at the degree of the Nodes, and none in the travel houses. However, we do find violent Capricorn on the cusp of the ninth house (travel), while Aries is on the cusp of the twelfth (hospitals) and Scorpio on the cusp of the public seventh house.

Judy is a New Moon baby with both Sun and Moon elevated in the tenth house (a saver). The Part of Fortune rises in the first house (a protection) and is in exact sextile to benefic Venus, ruler

97

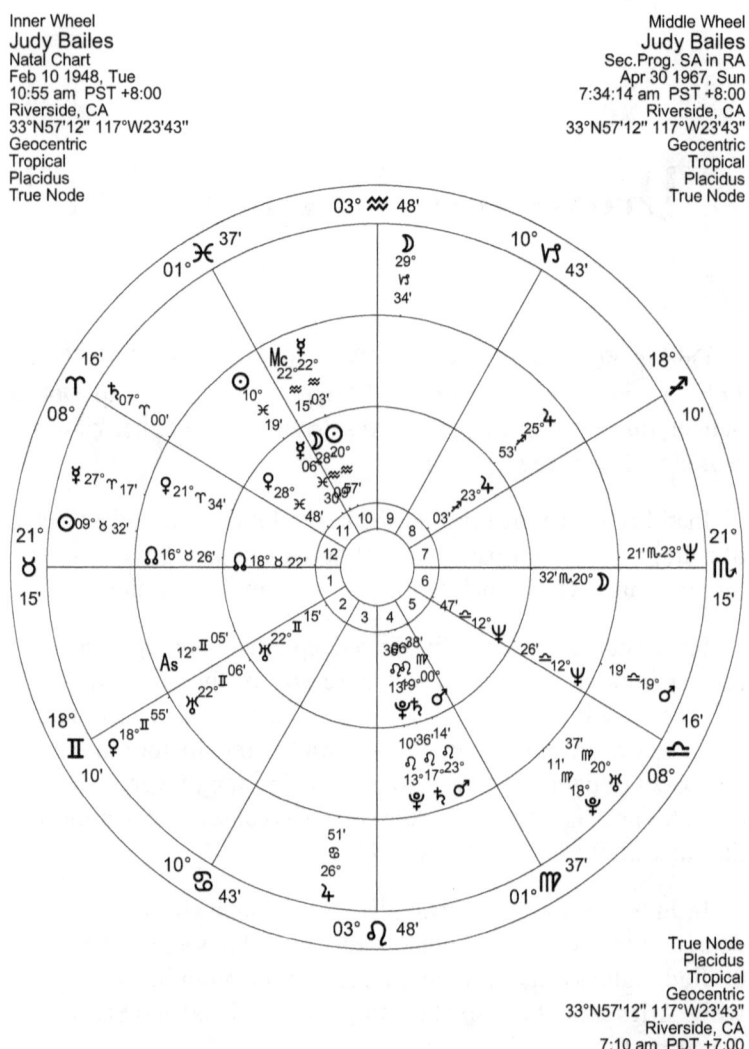

of the critical Ascendant (another saver). However, it is also in an exact square to the Moon, ruler of the third house of brothers and sisters, as well as of travel; her sister died in a car accident four years later.

All five so-called malefics are below the horizon (the personal self), and all are retrograde or introspective, so the events had a deep traumatic effect on her.

In the fourth house we find a Pluto-Saturn (of falls) conjunction in Leo (the back), while Mars (cuts and the nose) is also posited there.

Mars, co-ruler of the seventh (public) house and ruler of the twelfth of hospitals, is trine the Part of Surgery and opposition Mercury (ribs) of transportation.

Jupiter is in its own sign, Sagittarius of transportation, in the eighth house of surgery, which it rules in this chart. It is quincunx the Ascendant (physical body) and in close opposition to rising Uranus (the unexpected), ruling the line of destiny, with both of them square Venus, which is the fulcrum of the mutable cross.

Neptune in the sixth house of health and work is sesquisquare the Moon and Fortuna, sextile Pluto, and quincunx Part of Death.

The Part of Fatality at the cursed degree of Scorpio opposes the Ascendant from the sixth house and is conjunct the South Node.

The Part of Surgery is at a critical degree in the twelfth of hospitals, while the Part of Catastrophe is square Uranus and the Part of Peril opposes Venus and is square the Jupiter-Uranus opposition.

Fixed Stars
- Fortuna conjunct Alcyone (nature of Moon and Mars).
- Uranus conjunct Ensis (nature of Mars and Moon).
- Pluto conjunct Acubens (nature of Saturn and Mercury).
- Saturn conjunct Algenubi (nature of Saturn and Mars).

- Neptune conjunct Algorab, nature of Mars and Saturn.
- Jupiter conjunct Lesath, nature of Mercury and Mars.
- Sun conjunct Nashira, nature of Saturn and Jupiter.
- Mercury conjunct Skat, nature of Saturn and Jupiter.
- Venus conjunct Scheat, nature of Mars and Mercury.

Thus we have an emphasis on Saturn (falls), Mars (cuts and the nose), Mercury (ribs, transportation), and Jupiter (in this map, surgery).

Preceding Eclipses

- June 14, 1965, partial lunar eclipse at 22 Sagittarius 30, in natal eighth house, conjunct Jupiter, ruler of the eighth, opposition Uranus (the unexpected), squared Part of Catastrophe and Part of Peril.
- November 23, 1965, annular solar eclipse at 00 Sagittarius 40, square Mars, ruler of seventh and twelfth.
- May 20, 1966, annular solar eclipse at 28 Taurus 56, in natal first house (personal focus), conjunct Fortuna (a saver).
- November 12, 1966, total solar eclipse at 19 Scorpio 45, in natal sixth house of work and health, conjunct South Node and Part of Fatality, square Sun and Saturn.
- April 26, 1962 (four days before the event), total lunar eclipse at 3 Scorpio 00, in the sixth of health, square Midheaven, trine Mercury of transportation.

Primary Directions

- Mars at 19 Virgo 38, semisextile natal Saturn, sextile Part of Fatality.
- Moon at 17 Pisces 07, a critical degree.
- Part of Peril at 15 Libra 37, semisquare natal Mars.
- Part of Surgery at 28 Taurus 55, conjunct natal Fortuna, sextile natal Venus and square natal Moon.
- Part of Illness at 22 Gemini 03, conjunct natal Uranus, square natal Part of Catastrophe.

Converse Directions
- Converse Saturn at 0 Leo 10, semisextile natal Mars.
- Converse Neptune at 23 Virgo 50, square natal Jupiter.
- Converse Jupiter at 4 Sagittarius 03, a critical degree.
- Converse Moon at 9 Aquarius 13, a critical degree, square natal Part of Surgery.
- Converse Venus at 9 Pisces 51, sextile natal Part of Surgery.
- Converse Part of Surgery at 21 Aries 01, semisquare natal Mercury.

Tertiary Directions
- Tertiary Ascendant in natal eighth house at a critical degree in violent Capricorn exactly opposed by tertiary retrograde Uranus (also critical), both of them square tertiary Part of Surgery and Part Catastrophe.
- Tertiary Saturn, ruler of the tertiary Ascendant, is in the tertiary Eighth of surgery, conjunct natal Mars, opposition natal Mercury.
- Tertiary Mars, ruling tertiary fourth house, square natal Mars and Mercury.
- Tertiary Moon in tertiary sixth house rules the public tertiary seventh house.
- Tertiary Moon in close opposition to natal and tertiary Jupiter, conjunct natal Uranus, trine tertiary Sun.
- Tertiary Uranus quincunx tertiary Mars.
- Tertiary Venus in tertiary ninth of travel at same degree as natal Nodes.
- Tertiary Neptune (fog) at critical degree in tertiary ninth, sesquisquare natal Moon, trine tertiary Part of Death.
- Tertiary Mercury in tertiary tenth; trine natal Uranus, tertiary Moon, and Part of Peril; sextile natal and tertiary Jupiter.
- Tertiary Sun, ruler tertiary eighth, trine natal Sun (a saver),

quincunx natal Venus and Fortuna.
- Tertiary Pluto in tertiary eighth house conjunct natal Saturn and tertiary Fortuna.
- Tertiary Part of Peril quincunx natal Part of Peril, trine tertiary Sun.

Secondary Progressions
- Progressed Ascendant trine natal and progressed Neptune.
- Progressed Mars conjunct progressed IC, trine natal Jupiter.
- Progressed Mercury trine progressed Uranus.
- Progressed Venus semisquare natal Mercury.

Transits
- Transiting Sun in natal twelfth house of hospitals, at a critical degree and exactly conjunct natal Part of Surgery, sesquisquare natal Part of Peril, and sextile progressed Sun.
- Transiting Mercury, also in natal twelfth, sextile natal Venus and Fortuna (a saver), sextile progressed Part of Surgery, opposition tertiary Sun.
- Transiting Venus conjunct natal second cusp/opposition natal eighth cusp at same degree as natal Nodes, square tertiary Venus, in tertiary sixth house.
- Transiting Jupiter at a critical degree in natal third house trine natal Venus (setting off natal cross), quincunx natal Sun, sesquisquare natal Mercury, quincunx natal and tertiary Jupiter, square tertiary Sun, sextile tertiary Moon.
- Transiting Pluto at same degree as natal Nodes, quincunx natal Uranus and Jupiter, conjunct tertiary Venus, quincunx progressed Fortuna.
- Transiting retrograde Uranus opposition natal Venus, semisextile natal Mercury, quincunx natal Sun, square natal Uranus and Jupiter, tertiary Moon and Jupiter.
- Transiting retrograde Mars semisextile natal Part of Fatality and tertiary Venus, trine progressed Fortuna, opposition

progressed Fortuna, conjunct tertiary MC, opposition tertiary fourth cusp and progressed Venus.
- Transiting retrograde Neptune quincunx natal Uranus and tertiary Moon, sextile natal and tertiary Jupiter and natal Part of Catastrophe, and square progressed Mercury, Mars, MC-IC.
- Transiting Saturn conjunct natal twelfth cusp opposition natal, progressed, and tertiary Neptune; semisquare natal Ascendant; sesquisquare progressed Mars and fourth cusp.
- Transiting Nodes at natal Mercury degree.
- Transiting Moon quincunx natal Mars, tertiary Uranus, and seventh cusp; semisextile tertiary Ascendant; trine tertiary Part of Surgery.

Chapter 13

Truck Rollover

This young man was anticipating his wedding day as he drove his semi-truck along the highway (he married a few months after the event). Apparently the truck hit a pothole, causing the load to shift and the truck to roll over into a ditch at approximately 3:00 pm on August 8, 1975, at latitude 41N.

He suffered a broken back and a concussion from a skull fracture, and his right-eye vision was blinded by broken glass.

Violent Aries is on the Ascendant, but there are no planets in violent signs and none at the degree of the lunar Nodes.

Mars, ruler of the Ascendant, is part of a four-planet grouping, plus Fortuna in the fifth house in Leo (the spine). It is afflicted by its conjunction to Pluto, both of them co-ruling the intercepted public seventh house. This is a bowl pattern with Jupiter as a high focus planet, ruling the eighth house of surgery and the ninth of travel. Although posited in the second house, it is near the travel third cusp, void of course, detrimented, conjunct the Part of Fatality, and opposition the Part of Peril.

Mercury, as part of the Leo stellium, is ruler of the third and also the sixth of work and health. It straddles the fifth cusp, tying it in to both the fourth and fifth houses. It is conjunct Fortuna and trine the Moon (two savers).

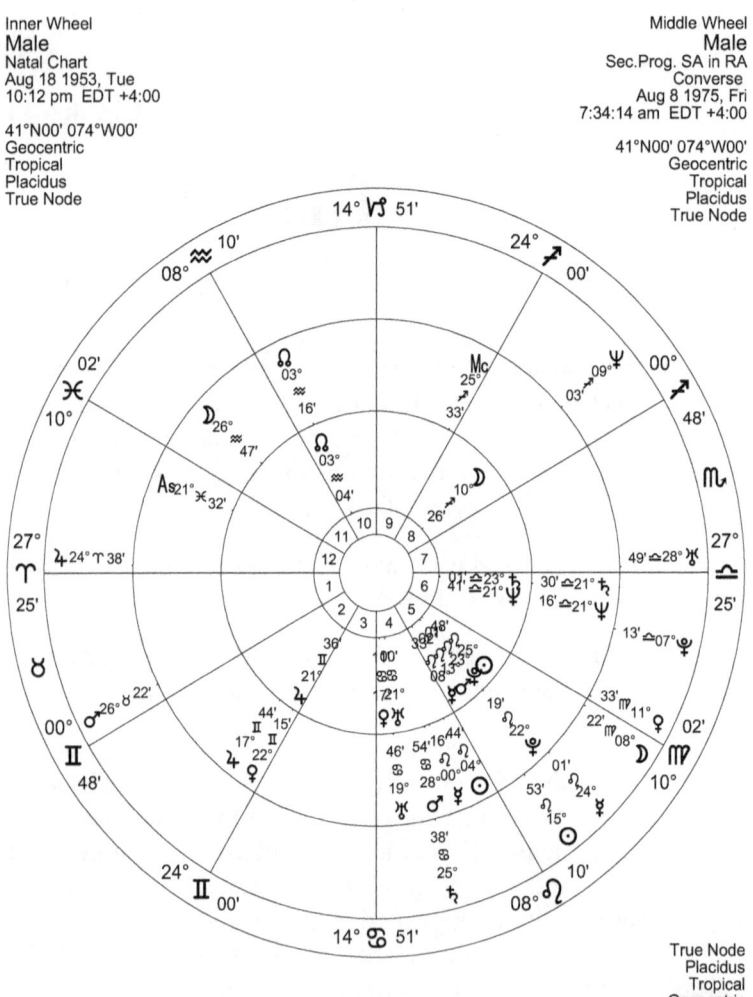

The Sun is besieged by Pluto and Neptune, while Venus, co-ruler of the intercepted first house and true ruler of the public seventh, is afflicted, not only by its conjunction to Uranus in the fourth but also by its square to Neptune and exalted Saturn posited in the sixth of work and health.

The functioning Moon, in the surgery eighth house, is disposited by Jupiter, ruler of the eighth. It is trine Fortuna (a saver), trine Mars, widely opposition Jupiter, and trine the Part of Death.

The Point of Accident is posited in the fourth house, conjunct the South Node for a loss (the eyesight), and trine the Moon.

Fixed Stars
- Jupiter conjunct Prima Hyadum (nature of Saturn and Mercury).
- Venus conjunct Wasat (nature of Saturn).
- Uranus is conjunct Pollux (nature of Mars).
- Mercury and the fifth cusp conjunct South Ascellus, threatening the eyes (nature of Mars and Sun).
- Mars conjunct Acubens (nature of Saturn and Mercury).
- Sun conjunct Adhafera and Alphard (nature of Saturn, Venus, and Mercury).
- Neptune conjunct Denebola (nature of Saturn and Venus).
- Moon conjunct Rastaban (nature of Saturn and Venus).

The more fixed stars involved, the more drastic and lasting the effect.

Preceding Eclipses
- June 20, 1974 total solar eclipse at 28 Gemini 30 in natal third, opposition Part of Peril, semisquare Mars and Fortuna.
- November 29, 1974, total lunar eclipse at 7 Gemini 00 semisextile Part of Surgery, semisquare Uranus, opposition Moon.

- December 13, 1974, partial solar eclipse at 21 Sagittarius in natal ninth house, opposition Jupiter, quincunx Uranus, trine the Sun and Pluto, sextile the Saturn-Neptune conjunction.
- May 11, 1975, partial solar eclipse at 19 Taurus 59 in natal first house (personal focus), semisextile Jupiter, sextile Venus and Uranus, square Pluto and the Sun, quincunx the Neptune-Saturn conjunction, trine the Point of Greatest Danger.
- May 25, 1975, total lunar eclipse at 5 Sagittarius 00 in natal eighth house, trine Mercury, semisquare Neptune and Saturn, quincunxed the Part of Surgery, sesquisquare Uranus.

Primary Directions
- Jupiter at 13 Cancer 09, a critical degree.
- Venus at 8 Leo 51, conjunct natal Mercury and fifth cusp.
- Mars at 4 Virgo 42, a critical degree.
- Uranus at 12 Leo 39, conjunct natal Fortuna.
- Sun at 17 Virgo 27, a critical degree, sextile natal Venus (a saver).
- Neptune at 13 Scorpio 20, square natal Mars.
- Part of Peril at 17 Capricorn 47, opposition natal Venus.
- Part of Death at 9 Taurus 44, a critical degree.
- Fortuna at 4 Virgo 42, a critical degree.

Converse Directions
- Converse Jupiter at 29 Taurus 51, conjunct the Pleiades, giving something to cry about.
- Converse Venus at 25 Gemini 33, sextile natal Sun (a saver).
- Converse Mars at 21 Cancer 24, conjunct natal Uranus, semisextile natal Jupiter.
- Converse Uranus at 29 Gemini 21, out of rope.
- Converse Pluto at 1 Leo 23, conjunct natal South Node, for a loss.

- Converse Neptune at 0 Libra 02, a critical degree.
- Converse Saturn at 1 Libra 19, at the same degree as the lunar Nodes.
- Converse Moon at 18 Scorpio 52, quincunx natal Part of Death.
- Converse Part of Peril at 4 Sagittarius 34, a critical degree.
- Converse Part of Catastrophe at 1 Pisces 17, the same degree as natal lunar Nodes.

Tertiary Directions
- Four-planet grouping in Cancer with the dispositor Moon in the tertiary seventh house, void of course.
- Tertiary Ascendant in violent Capricorn square natal Ascendant, quincunx natal Moon.
- Tertiary Pluto, ruler of the tertiary line of destiny, conjunct tertiary Moon in the tertiary public seventh house, sesquisquare tertiary Mars; the latter is in violent Capricorn in the tertiary twelfth of hospitals, ruling tertiary third, opposition natal Part of Surgery, sesquisquare natal Pluto.
- Tertiary Jupiter conjunct tertiary sixth cusp and Mercury, both opposition tertiary Mars; trine tertiary Saturn and Part of Catastrophe; semisextile natal Point of Greatest Danger; square tertiary Part of Peril.
- Tertiary South Node and Venus conjunct natal Venus, square natal Part of Death.
- Tertiary Sun trine natal and tertiary Neptune, conjunct tertiary Part of Fatality in tertiary fifth house, opposition natal Moon, semisextile natal fourth cusp.
- Tertiary Neptune in Mercury-ruled tertiary eighth house exactly conjunct natal Saturn, trine natal Jupiter, quincunx natal Part of Catastrophe.

Secondary Progressions
- Progressed Ascendant semisextile natal Ascendant (a saver).

- Progressed Sun semisquare natal South Node.
- Progressed Mars trine natal Part of Peril.
- Progressed third and ninth cusps are critical, square progressed Part of Catastrophe.
- Progressed Jupiter conjunct natal third cusp, trine progressed Saturn for a number of years.
- Progressed Moon for August 1975 was critical, conjunct progressed Mercury, semisextile natal and tertiary Venus (he had a progressed New Moon the month before, indicating a new path in life).
- Progressed Moon conjunct Point of Danger, semisquare Point of Accident, trine progressed Part of Peril.
- Progressed Fortuna moving from a conjunction to the progressed Ascendant to a sextile of the progressed Part of Surgery.

Transits

- Transiting Sun conjunct natal Venus and Mars, opposition tertiary Part of Death.
- Transiting Mercury, at a critical degree, conjunct natal, progressed, and tertiary Pluto; sextile natal Jupiter; semisextile natal, progressed, and tertiary Uranus.
- Transiting retrograde Venus conjunct natal sixth cusp, square natal Moon and tertiary Sun, sesquisquare natal and tertiary Ascendants.
- Transiting Pluto in natal sixth house square natal Part of Surgery, opposition tertiary Fortuna, square tertiary Mars.
- Transiting Uranus opposition natal Ascendant, quincunx progressed Ascendant, square tertiary Ascendant, semisquare tertiary eighth cusp.
- Transiting retrograde Neptune conjunct natal Moon in natal eighth house, trine natal Mercury, quincunx progressed Part of Death, trine tertiary Fortuna.
- Transiting Jupiter in natal twelfth house opposition natal and progressed Neptune-Saturn conjunction and tertiary

Neptune; trine natal and progressed Pluto, natal Sun, natal Part of Peril, tertiary Pluto, tertiary Sun, progressed Mars.
- Transiting Mars in natal first house squares natal Sun, tertiary Moon, and progressed Mars.
- Transiting Saturn conjunct natal and progressed Uranus, semisextile natal Sun, square natal Ascendant, square all three Neptunes and natal and progressed Saturn; semisextile progressed Mars.
- Transiting South Node conjunct progressed Ascendant, at same degree as natal Ascendant.
- Transiting Moon at 4 Virgo 15 at a critical degree, semisextile tertiary Part of Peril and progressed fourth cusp, opposition tertiary Part of Catastrophe.

Chapter 13

Head-on Collision

This chart is a companion to that of A. E. Chabot (my father) in chapter 4. Out of the four persons involved in the event, my mother (Beatrice Chabot) was the only one who survived. She said that just before the accident happened she saw a ball of fire coming down the road toward them.

She immediately knew realized that something was about to happen and decided she had better go to sleep. Thus, she was in a semi-trance and limp when the taxi came speeding around the curve and hit their car head-on.

Mother suffered a concussion, a fractured cheekbone, and almost lost the sight in her left eye. As with my father, all the damage was to the left side of her body. She had a broken arm, broken ribs, and a punctured lung, and was left with a bent bone in her leg.

Within a week of the event her stomach ulcers ruptured, and she hemorrhaged for two days. She was losing blood faster than they could transfuse it, and she was too weak for surgery. But she survived all of that.

I had experienced a vision of the accident about five years before the event and knew that my mother would survive. The only part of the vision that confused me was that my mother kept screaming that she was drowning, but later was not associated with the vision. However, with drainage tubes in her lung, a catheter tube, and the bleeding ulcer, she was literally drowning in her own body fluids.

In her natal chart we find no planets in violent signs. The lunar Nodes are critical and at the same degree as the Ascendant, promising a personal, physical tragedy.

Jupiter, co-ruler of the Ascendant and ruler of the fourth of travel and foreign countries, rises in the map, a saver as it protects the physical body when posited in the first house. It is square a retrograde Uranus, ruler of the twelfth of hospitals and sorrows, and in wide opposition to Mars, co-ruler of the surgery eighth (she had many surgeries during her life).

Neptune, ruler of the Ascendant, is conjunct Venus in the fourth house, with both of them in quincunx aspect to Saturn in the twelfth.

The functioning Moon is also in the twelfth house, sextile Uranus, square the Sun (ruler of the sixth of health), and quincunx the seventh-house Mars (open enemies). Mars, the planet of surgery, is also co-ruler of the eighth of surgery and co-ruler of the intercepted Aries in the physical first house.

In the third house of short trips we find Mercury strong in its own travel sign of Gemini, conjunct Pluto, opposition Uranus of sudden, unexpected events, and square Jupiter, ruler of distant places (the event happened on a short trip at latitude 46N).

The Sun, ruling her sixth of health, is void of course and receives the semisquare from the critical South Node (I call it the robber) and the square from the Moon. It is opposed by the Part of Death and Part of Fatality, both posited in the eighth house, as are Peril Mars and the Point of Accident.

There are two Parts of Peril in the chart: Peril Pluto is conjunct the Parts of Surgery and Widowhood, while the Point of Greatest Danger falls in the ninth conjunct the Part of Fortune.

Venus, the lesser benefic, is besieged by Neptune and Mars and co-rules the seventh of partners and open enemies (those who meet you head-on). It is in a wide trine to the rising Jupiter (a saver) but quincunx the twelfth-house Saturn (her partner's house of health).

Fixed Stars
- Sun conjunct Alcyone (nature of Mars and Moon).
- Mercury conjunct Rigel (nature of Mars and Jupiter).
- Pluto conjunct Bellatrix (nature of Mars and Mercury).
- Mars conjunct Markeb (nature of Saturn and Jupiter).
- Uranus conjunct Aculeus (nature of Mars and Moon).
- Moon conjunct Deneb and Algedi (nature of Saturn and Mercury).

Primary Directions
- Sun at 28 Cancer 10, square natal Mars.
- Neptune at 3 Virgo 10, square the Point of Greatest Danger, sextile natal eighth cusp.
- Mars at 29 Virgo 05, out of rope, and sextile natal Part of Widowhood.
- Uranus at 25 Aquarius 48, square natal Part of Death and semisquare natal Part of Fatality.
- Moon advances to 24 Aries 06, trine natal Uranus and square natal Part of Surgery.
- Part of Fatality at 26 Capricorn 45, a critical degree.
- Part of Surgery at 25 Virgo 50, sextile natal Part of Fatality.
- Widowhood Uranus at 29 Virgo 07, the fatal degree.
- Widowhood Saturn at 13 Virgo 43, same degree as the lunar Nodes, and semisquare natal Mars.
- Peril Mars at 3 Capricorn 12, semisextile Point of Danger.

Converse Directions
- Converse Sun at 26 Pisces 00, sesquisquare the Point of Accident, trine natal Part of Surgery.

- Converse Mars at 26 Leo 35 conjunct natal Part of Surgery.
- Converse Uranus at 23 Libra 38, trine natal Moon.
- Converse Part of Fatality at 29 Virgo 35, sextile natal Part of Surgery.
- Converse Widowhood Uranus at 26 Taurus 57, conjunct natal Sun.
- Widowhood Saturn at 11 Cancer 33, conjunct natal fifth cusp, trine Point of Accident, semisextile natal Part of Catastrophe.
- Part of Catastrophe at 9 Leo 59, a critical degree, trine natal Fortuna.
- Fortuna at 8 Libra 17, conjunct fixed star Vindiematrix, Star of Widowhood.

Tertiary Diretions

- Tertiary Ascendant opposition natal Saturn, trine natal Fortuna (a saver), semisextile tertiary Mercury and Neptune at their midpoint, quincunx tertiary Part of Fatality.
- Tertiary Venus, ruler of tertiary fourth house, rises in the tertiary first (a saver), exactly semisextile tertiary Pluto, trine natal Uranus and tertiary Neptune, ruler of tertiary eighth and ninth conjunct the tertiary twelfth cusp of hospitals and the natal fifth cusp of pleasure, opposition tertiary Part of Fatality, trine tertiary Part of Catastrophe.
- Tertiary lunar Nodes at the same degree as natal Mars.
- Tertiary Pluto opposition natal Uranus, square tertiary Sun, semisextile natal Sun.
- Tertiary Sun trine natal Sun and Mars (a saver), quincunx tertiary retrograde Saturn, which is conjunct tertiary South Node in the tertiary seventh, the latter quincunx natal Mars.
- Tertiary MC and IC are critical.
- Tertiary Jupiter, co-ruler of tertiary eighth and ninth Houses, conjunct the tertiary Moon in the tertiary eleventh of hopes and wishes for the future.
- Tertiary Jupiter square tertiary Mercury, opposition tertiary

Mars, in natal third house, conjunct natal Mercury and Neptune, semisextile natal Venus (a saver).
- Tertiary Moon exactly conjunct tertiary Part of Widowhood, opposition tertiary Mars, sextile tertiary Ascendant (a saver), square natal Ascendant.
- Tertiary Uranus critical, rules the tertiary seventh of partners, opposition tertiary Neptune and natal Venus and Neptune, square natal Peril Mars, semisextile natal Point of Greatest Danger.
- Tertiary Part of Fatality in tertiary sixth of health, sextile natal Point of Accident, conjunct natal eleventh cusp, square tertiary Ascendant-Descendant.

Preceding Eclipses
- January 14, 1964, partial solar eclipse at 23 Capricorn 43 opposition progressed Sun, semisextile natal Moon.
- June 10, 1964, partial solar eclipse at 19 Gemini 19 conjunct natal and progressed Pluto and progressed Ascendant.
- June 25, 1964, total lunar eclipse at 3 Capricorn 18 opposition natal and progressed Neptune and natal Venus, semisextile Point of Greatest Danger.
- July 9, 1964, partial solar eclipse at 17 Cancer 14 trine natal Jupiter, conjunct progressed Jupiter, semisextile natal and progressed Pluto.
- December 4, 1964, partial solar eclipse at 11 Sagittarius 56 sextile natal Part of Catastrophe, squared Widowhood Saturn, conjunct progressed Part of Catastrophe, opposition natal Mercury.
- December 19, 1964, total lunar eclipse at 27 Gemini 00 in natal fourth, square natal Mars, semisextile natal Widowhood Uranus and Sun, quincunx progressed Part of Fatality.

Secondary Progressions
- Progressed Ascendant conjunct natal Pluto, square natal Jupiter.

- Progressed fourth cusp sextile progressed Pluto, semisquare progressed Neptune.
- Progressed Mars trine progressed Pluto, trine natal fourth cusp.
- Progressed Venus at same degree as progressed lunar Nodes.
- Progressed Moon for April 1965 at 15 Taurus 17 semisextile natal Mercury (a saver), with progressed Fortuna square progressed eighth cusp, and moving to the sextile of natal Saturn.

Transits

- Transiting Sun conjunct natal Sun, trine tertiary Sun (a saver), trine natal Mars, square natal Moon, sextile progressed Sun (a saver).
- Transiting Moon opposition natal Sun.
- Transiting Moon square natal Moon, sextile tertiary Sun and natal Mars.
- Transiting Venus conjunct natal third cusp, semisextile natal Neptune and quincunx tertiary Saturn, conjunct tertiary Jupiter and Moon (a saver), opposition natal Point of Greatest Danger, semisextiles tertiary Part of Death, trine natal and progressed Saturn.
- Transiting Jupiter conjunct tertiary Jupiter and Moon (a saver) in natal third, trine natal and progressed Saturn.
- Transiting Uranus, Mars and Pluto (all conjunct in Virgo) in natal sixth house with Pluto at the degree of the lunar Nodes, opposition Ascendant. All conjunct natal Widowhood Saturn, square natal Mercury, natal and progressed Pluto, progressed Ascendant and tertiary Mars, trine the progressed Moon, opposition natal Jupiter, sextile progressed Mercury and natal Widowhood Saturn, quincunx natal Saturn, conjunct tertiary Mercury, trine tertiary Part of Fatality, sextile tertiary Neptune, quincunx tertiary seventh house cusp.

- Transiting Neptune opposition natal Sun, conjunct natal Part of Death in natal eighth house, conjunct tertiary Part of Catastrophe, quincunx tertiary Fortuna, quincunx natal and progressed Pluto, quincunx progressed Ascendant, trine natal and progressed Jupiter.
- Transiting Mercury at fatal degree semisquare natal Mercury, quincunx natal Mars, sextile tertiary Saturn.
- Transiting Saturn conjunct natal Ascendant and Jupiter, square natal Mercury, square natal and progressed Pluto, square progressed Ascendant-Descendant, opposition natal Widowhood Saturn, trine progressed Widowhood Saturn, in tertiary eighth house, trine tertiary Part of Catastrophe, square tertiary Mars and Pluto.

Chapter 14
Fall from Motorcycle

On 30 April 1973, at approximately 7:00 pm, latitude 34N, as his father was giving my grandson a ride on a three-wheeled sand motorcycle up a steep incline, the cycle apparently hit something that caused them to go tumbling down the hill.

His father took him home, and at first he seemed to be all right. After a while, however, the boy became nauseated and drowsy, so his parents took him to the hospital. Nothing drastic showed up in the tests and x-rays but they kept him overnight as a precaution.

Early the next morning he was found to have no blood pressure or radial pulse, and he was cyanotic. He was in shock and, by some clinical definition, he had died. The doctor in charge decided to take a chance and gave him a shot, which revived him. As the doctor later explained to my daughter (his mother), when children lose a lot of blood, the reaction is for the muscles to contract to push the blood to the heart where it is needed. In doing so the fluid had also been pushed out of his lungs and, upon reviving, he reswallowed it, which burned his lungs and bronchial tubes.

He was rushed to surgery, where they found his small intestine had been cut in half, which they had missed in the examination because the blood was pooling in the back instead of in the front abdomen, as is usually the case. The surgery started at 8:25 am and was completed at 10:20 am; he "died" three times, but was revived each time.

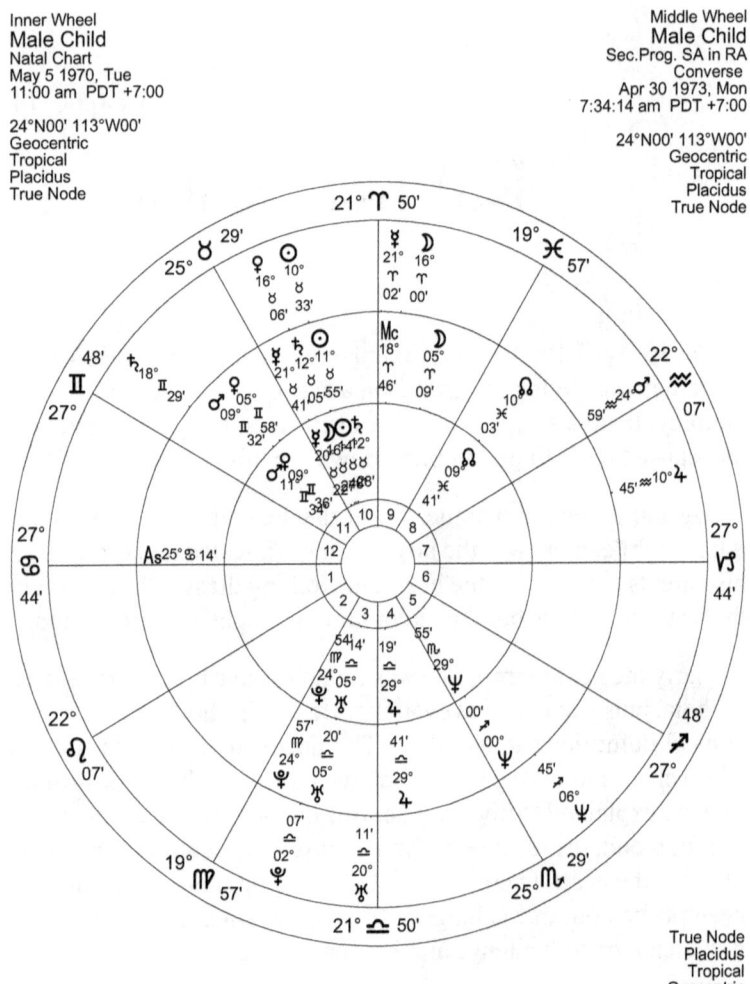

Because of the lung problem, he was put on a breathing machine and kept in the intensive care unit. He had a pediatrician, a pulmonary specialist and a neurosurgeon in attendance.

On May 5 he had his third birthday. His body chemistry was still out of balance, and the prognosis for recovery was still poor. Then one morning he awoke and asked for food; recovery was completed by May 23, when he was finally discharged and went home to his family.

This is a New Moon baby with a Taurus stellium in the tenth house. In this chart the Sun is applying to the conjunction of the exalted Moon, ruler of the Ascendant. The chart lacks fire.

Venus and retrograde Mercury are in mutual reception (a saver), but Peril Saturn is conjunct the Part of Catastrophe, quincunx Mercury, and sesquisquare the Point of Accident.

The only planet in a violent sign is retrograde Neptune, posited in the fifth of amusement and ruling the travel ninth.

Jupiter, ruler of the sixth of health, is posited in the fourth house, retrograde and at the out-of-rope 29 degrees, exactly square Fortuna in the first, trine Part of Surgery, and semi-sextile the 29-degree retrograde Neptune in the fifth House of pleasure. The other two planets—Pluto and Uranus—posited in the third, are also retrograde, making all four planets below the horizon retrograde.

Pluto is in Virgo, the sign ruling the intestines, posited at the midpoint of Ascendant Peril Saturn, Fortuna and Neptune, square the Part of Surgery.

Uranus in the travel third rules the eighth of surgery. It is trine Venus and Mars, sesquisquare Mercury, and rules the third.

Mars is conjunct Venus in the lung and breathing sign of Gemini, exactly conjunct the Anti-Vertex (physical manifestation), widely square Pluto, semisextile Saturn, Sun, and Moon, and mutual reception Venus; the latter's degree, back in its own sign, is critical.

The Ascendant and Fortuna are trine Neptune (unseen things), while the Point of greatest Danger is sextile them and opposition Neptune.

The Point of Accident is square the Taurus stellium and sextile Uranus in the travel third.

Fixed Stars
- Sun and Saturn conjunct Menkar (nature of Saturn.
- Venus conjunct Aldeberan (nature of Mars.

There is not much pressure from the fixed stars (a help).

Primary Directions
- Ascendant and Peril Saturn at 1 Leo 08, sesquisquare natal Saturn.
- Uranus at 8 Libra 12, conjunct fixed star Vindiematrix, nature of Saturn and Mercury, and at same degree as the lunar Nodes.
- Mars at 14 Gemini 30, semisextile natal Sun, sesquisquare natal Jupiter.
- Part of Fatality at 28 Cancer 43, conjunct natal Ascendant.
- Part of Surgery at 1 Cancer 57, sextile radix Part of Death.
- Part of Catastrophe at 21 Sagittarius 36, conjunct natal Peril Uranus.
- Part of Peril at 24 Sagittarius 01, square natal Pluto.

Converse Directions
- Converse Ascendant at 25 Cancer 16, conjunct radix Part of Fatality.
- Converse Pluto at 21 Virgo 59, square natal Peril Uranus.

- Converse Jupiter at 26 libra 29, critical degree, quincunx Point of Greatest Danger.
- Converse Saturn at 9 Taurus 27, critical degree, conjunct mutual reception Venus.
- Converse Sun at 1 Taurus 52, conjunct natal Part of Death.
- Converse Mercury at 17 Taurus 26, quincunx natal fourth cusp, semisextile natal Midheaven.
- Converse Mars at 8 Gemini 38, at same degree as lunar Nodes.
- Converse Fortuna at 26 Cancer 53, critical degree, sextile Point of Greatest Danger.
- Converse Part of Peril at 18 Sagittarius 09, conjunct radix Part of Catastrophe.

Tertiary Directions
- Tertiary Ascendant conjunct natal second cusp, opposition natal eighth cusp, square natal Mercury and Pluto.
- Tertiary Sun, ruler of tertiary Ascendant, conjunct natal Venus, Mars and Anti-Vertex; trine natal Part of Catastrophe, semisquare tertiary retrograde Uranus; sextile tertiary Part of Death.
- Tertiary Moon (exalted in Taurus like the natal Moon) conjunct tertiary MC in the ninth of travel, conjunct natal Saturn, square tertiary Ascendant, ruler of the tertiary twelfth house of hospitals.
- Tertiary Mars (at the out-of-rope 29 degrees) conjunct natal Part of Surgery, trine natal Jupiter, quincunx natal and tertiary Neptune, co-ruler of tertiary fourth, ruler of the ninth of travel.
- Tertiary Venus semisextile natal Venus and Mars, sextile mutual reception Venus and tertiary Moon (a saver).
- Tertiary Part of Fatality exactly conjunct natal Part of Fatality, sextile natal and tertiary Pluto, square natal and tertiary Jupiter, rules the tertiary fifth house of pleasure, co-rules the tertiary eighth house.

- Tertiary Neptune (still retrograde and at 29 degrees) in the tertiary fourth, rules the tertiary eighth house of surgery.
- Tertiary Saturn conjunct tertiary Mercury, natal Moon and Sun.
- Tertiary Mercury exactly conjunct natal Moon, trine natal and tertiary Jupiter.
- There are two Parts of Peril: Part of Peril Jupiter in tertiary sixth house of health, Part of Peril Neptune in tertiary public seventh house.
- Tertiary retrograde Jupiter at a critical degree, quincunx the natal Point of greatest Danger, sesquisquare natal Mars.
- The tertiary lunar Nodes at the same degree as natal Point of Accident.
- Tertiary Part of Catastrophe opposition natal Mars and tertiary Part of Death, semisquare natal Jupiter, sesquisquare natal Fortuna.
- Tertiary Part of Catastrophe exactly semisextile natal Mercury, sextile mutual reception Mercury.

Preceding Eclipses
- January 30, 1972, partial lunar eclipse at 9 Leo 00, critical degree, sextile natal Venus, square mutual reception Venus, semisquare natal and progressed Pluto.
- July 10, 1972, total solar eclipse at 18 Cancer 37 in natal twelfth house, quincunx natal Part of Catastrophe, sextile natal and progressed Mercury.
- July 26, 1972, partial lunar eclipse at 2 Aquarius 00 opposition progressed Part of Peril Saturn; conjunct progressed Part of Catastrophe; semisquare natal Moon, progressed Sun, and Mercury.
- January 4, 1973, partial lunar eclipse at 14 Capricorn 08 sesquisquare natal and progressed Neptune; trine natal and progressed Sun, natal Moon and progressed Mercury.

Secondary Progressions
- Progressed Sun conjunct natal Moon.
- Progressed retrograde Mercury semisextile progressed MC, quincunx progressed fourth cusp.
- Progressed Venus conjunct progressed Mars.
- Progressed Ascendant conjunct natal Fortuna.
- Progressed Moon semisextile natal Sun, sesquisquare natal and progressed Jupiter, semisextile progressed Sun and natal Moon.
- Progressed Fortuna semisextile natal Ascendant and Part of Peril Saturn.

Transits
- Transiting Sun at a critical degree conjunct mutual reception Venus and semisextile natal Venus (both savers); sesquisquare natal, progressed and tertiary Pluto.
- Transiting Mercury conjunct natal MC, opposition natal fourth cusp, sextile tertiary Part of Death, trine natal Part of Catastrophe.
- Transiting Saturn opposition natal Part of Catastrophe, conjunct tertiary eleventh cusp and tertiary Part of Death, sextile natal MC, semisextile tertiary Ascendant.
- Transiting retrograde Pluto conjunct natal, progressed and tertiary Uranus in natal third house; sesquisquare natal Moon, progressed Sun, and tertiary Saturn and Mercury.
- Transiting retrograde Uranus quincunx natal and progressed Mercury.
- Transiting retrograde Mercury sextile natal, progressed, and tertiary Uranus; opposition natal Venus and tertiary Sun.
- Transiting Jupiter square natal Saturn, Sun, Moon, progressed Saturn and Sun, tertiary Moon, Saturn and Mercury; sesquisquare natal, progressed and tertiary Pluto.
- Transiting Mars quincunx natal, progressed and tertiary Pluto from natal and progressed eighth house; quincunx na-

tal and progressed Ascendants and Part of Peril Saturn; square natal, progressed, and tertiary Neptune.
- Transiting Moon in natal and progressed ninth houses conjunct natal MC, semisextile natal Moon and progressed Sun, sextile progressed Moon.

Chapter 15

Fall Off Cliff

The main interest of this talented, artistic man (Jay) is sculpting in bronze, and his work is in great demand. On November 29, 1969, he and his brother and a number of friends were on a camping vacation in Tijuana, Mexico.

They set up camp at the edge of a cliff overlooking the ocean. Jay's brother was visiting another campsite while the rest of them were sitting around the campfire having a quiet discussion. At about 10:00 pm, a gust of wind blew the flames toward Jay, who jumped up and backed away—straight down over the cliff.

The others reacted immediately and went for Jay's brother, who had skidded down the cliffside in order to pull Jay back from the incoming tide, while some of the others went for help.

Jay was taken to the hospital with a frontal fracture of the right side of the skull and a concussion. To this day he has no true memory of the details of the accident. He also had a fractured pelvis and hip bone, which left one leg shorter than the other and which still gives him problems with his back. His right cheek bone was crushed, and the stitches became so infected that he almost lost the sight in his right eye.

When his parents finally managed to have him transferred to a U.S. hospital, the infection was cleared up, and he has only a slight facial scar as a reminder of his experience.

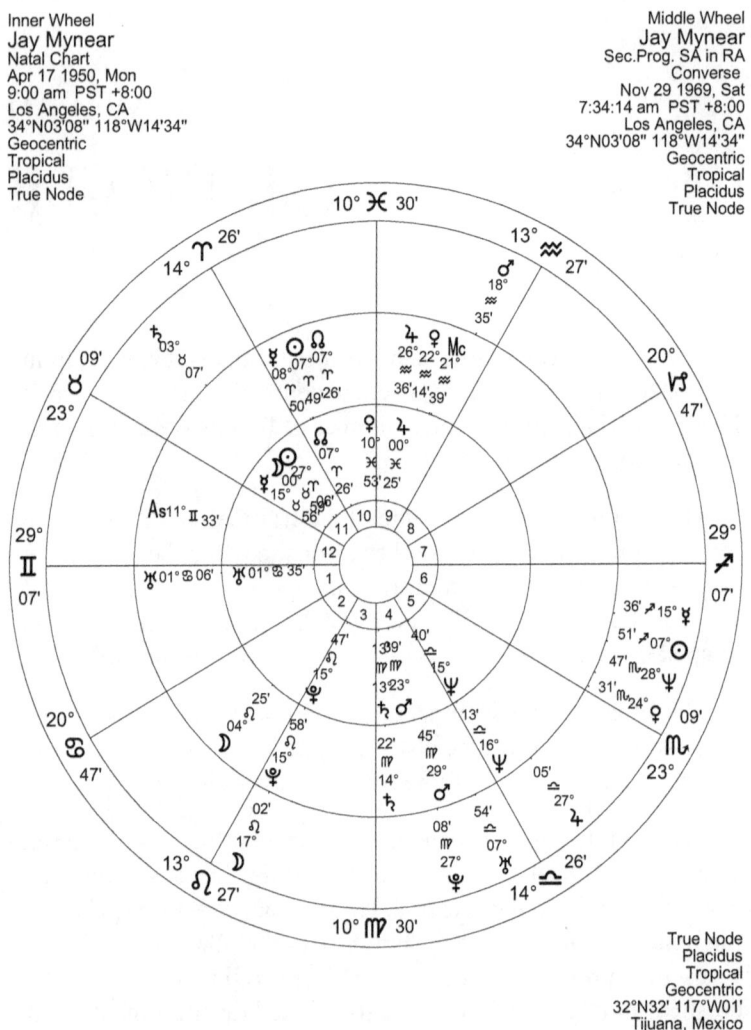

In his natal chart we find the out-of-rope degree (29) rising in the travel sign of Gemini. The Part of Peril sits on the Ascendant, waiting to be set off.

The only planet in a violent sign is the eleventh house Sun (friends), ruling the third, and there are no planets at the degree of the lunar Nodes.

Mercury, ruler of the Ascendant, is also in the eleventh house of circumstances beyond our control, exactly opposing Part of Fatality and applying to the conjunction of the Anti-Vertex (physical manifestation). It is quincunx retrograde Neptune in Libra, which straddles the fifth cusp of pleasure and rules the tenth of high places. Mercury is also square the third house retrograde Pluto.

In the fourth house, also Mercury-ruled, we find a Saturn-Mars conjunction, both of them retrograde and square the Ascendant. They are in trine aspect to Mercury and quincunx the Sun.

Jupiter (ruling the pelvis and the hip), the greater benefic, is conjunct Venus, the lesser benefic, in the ninth house of foreign countries. It is strong in its co-rulership of Pisces and is also dignified by being in its own house, while Venus is in its exaltation. Both are in an out-of-sign trine to the Ascendant—all savers!

Venus rules the fifth of pleasure (the camping vacation) and the twelfth of hospitals, with the cusp of the latter being conjunct the fixed star Caput Algol of the nature of Mars and Mercury, the two rulers of surgery.

Both Jupiter (hip and pelvis) and Venus (beauty) oppose the Saturn (falls)-Mars (the head) conjunction, sextile Mercury (ruler of the physical body and a saver), semisquare the Sun, and quincunx Pluto and Neptune.

The latter two thus form a yod with Venus with the point of outlet or manifestation being the Saturn-Mars conjunction.

Saturn rules the eighth of surgery and co-rules the ninth, while Mars rules the eleventh and co-rules the sixth of health.

Uranus (the unexpected), true ruler of the ninth house, rises in the first house of the chart (the physical body), accompanied by the Part of Fortune, which protects when in the Ascendant. Both are in trine aspect to the benefic Jupiter-Venus conjunction (a saver).

The exalted Moon in Taurus is sextile Jupiter and also sextile Venus, Uranus, and Fortuna (is at the midpoint of Jupiter and Uranus). While it could not prevent the event, the functioning Moon is a saver here—the "Thank The Lord" aspect of cosmobiology.

Fixed Stars
- Ascendant conjunct Menkalinan (nature of Mars and Mercury).
- Neptune and fifth cusp conjunct Seginus (nature of Mercury and Saturn).
- Sun conjunct Vindermatrix (nature of Mars and Moon).

There is less of a fixed star influence in this map, and thus less pressure.

Primary Directions
- Ascendant at 19 Cancer 51, semisextile natal Part of Surgery.
- Pluto at 6 Virgo 06, at the same degree as the lunar Nodes.
- Mars at 13 Libra 59, a critical degree, semisextile natal Saturn.
- Neptune at 6 Scorpio 42, at same degree as lunar Nodes.
- Jupiter at 20 Pisces 42, conjunct natal Part of Death.
- Venus at 1 Aries 13, square natal Uranus, setting off the trine between them.
- Sun at 17 Taurus 23, semisquare natal Fortuna.
- Moon at 20 Taurus 49, sextile natal Part of Death (he almost died).

- Mercury at 6 Gemini 14, at same degree as lunar Nodes.
- Part of Fatality at 6 Sagittarius 02, square lunar Nodes.
- Part of Death at 10 Aries 33, semisextile natal Venus.

Converse Directions
- Converse Uranus at 11 Gemini 16, square the natal MC and IC.
- Converse Pluto at 25 Cancer 28, sesquisquare natal Venus.
- Converse Jupiter at 10 Aquarius 04, semisextile natal Venus (a saver).
- Converse Venus at 20 Aquarius 35, semisextile natal Part of Death.
- Converse Sun at 6 Aries 55, at same degree as lunar Nodes.
- Converse Part of Catastrophe at 14 Leo 07, semisquare natal Ascendant.

Although there is much activity in the primary and converse directions, the aspects formed are mostly minor ones.

Tertiary Directions
- Tertiary Ascendant in natal ninth house of foreign countries, with its ruler, Neptune, in tertiary eighth.
- Co-ruler Jupiter rises in the tertiary first house (a saver) along with the North Node, rules the tertiary tenth of high places.
- A fixed T-cross in the chart with the Moon ruling the tertiary fifth of pleasure and square natal and tertiary Pluto, and trine natal Saturn and Mars; Moon is conjunct natal Mercury.
- Tertiary Mercury is sextile tertiary Jupiter, and both are quincunx natal and tertiary Pluto, with the outlet of the yod being the Venus-Mars conjunction in the twelfth of hospitals.
- Tertiary Uranus is in the tertiary fourth, conjunct the tertiary fifth, retrograde, trine the rising tertiary Jupiter and

natal Venus. It is at the same degree as the natal lunar Nodes and rules the tertiary twelfth house, and is opposition tertiary Mercury, ruler of the tertiary fourth, both of them square Saturn as the fulcrum of the cardinal T-cross.
- Tertiary Sun and Mercury are in violent Capricorn with tertiary Sun void of course in the tertiary chart.
- Tertiary Venus, ruling the tertiary eighth of surgery, in the tertiary twelfth in wide conjunction with tertiary Mars, co-ruler of the tertiary ninth house, opposition tertiary Part of Catastrophe.
- Tertiary Mars trine tertiary Fortuna in tertiary fourth house, conjunct natal Fortuna.
- Tertiary Part of Surgery trine tertiary Venus, semisextile tertiary fourth cusp, sesquisquare tertiary Mars, planet of surgery.
- Tertiary MC and IC square natal MC and IC (line of destiny); IC trine natal and tertiary Neptune, sextile natal and tertiary Pluto, semisextiles natal Mercury and tertiary Part of Peril.
- Tertiary Pluto, true ruler of the tertiary ninth, in tertiary sixth, retrograde, conjunct tertiary Part of Catastrophe, sextile tertiary Neptune as in the natal chart.

Secondary Progressions
- Progressed Venus conjunct progressed MC opposition progressed fourth cusp, semisextile progressed Jupiter and ninth cusp (a saver).
- Progressed Jupiter conjunct progressed ninth cusp.
- Progressed Part of Peril sesquisquare progressed Jupiter and ninth cusp.
- Progressed Moon same degree as progressed lunar Nodes.
- Progressed Fortuna at same degree as natal lunar Nodes.

Here we find fewer progressed aspects, and therefore less pressure.

Preceding Eclipses

- September 22, 1968, total solar eclipse at 29 Virgo 36 in the natal fourth house, square Ascendant-Descendant (personal focus), quincunx Sun.
- October 6, 1968, total lunar eclipse at 13 Aries 15, critical degree, opposition Neptune, trine Pluto, quincunx Part of Fatality.
- March 18, 1969, annular solar eclipse at 27 Pisces 16 semisextile Sun (a saver).
- April 2, 1969, partial lunar eclipse at 12 Libra 46 conjunct Neptune, quincunx Venus and Mercury, semisextile Saturn.
- August 27, 1969, partial lunar eclipse at 4 Pisces 06, critical degree, in natal ninth of travel and foreign countries, conjunct Jupiter, exactly opposition Part of Catastrophe.
- September 11, 1969, annular solar eclipse at 18 Virgo 48 between natal Saturn and Mars, square Part of Surgery, trine Mercury.
- September 25, 1969, partial lunar eclipse at 2 Aries 27 square Fortuna and Uranus, semisquare Mercury.

Transits

- Transiting Sun conjunct progressed Part of Fatality, square tertiary Ascendant, tertiary Jupiter, and natal Venus.
- Transiting Mercury opposition natal Part of Surgery; quincunx natal Mercury and tertiary Moon; sextile natal, progressed and tertiary Neptune; square natal and progressed Saturn and natal Mars; trine natal, progressed, and tertiary Pluto.
- Transiting Mars in natal ninth house and tertiary twelfth opposition natal, progressed, and tertiary Pluto; trine natal, progressed, and tertiary Neptune; quincunx natal and progressed Mars.
- Transiting retrograde Saturn conjunct natal Moon, sextile natal and progressed Jupiter, trine tertiary Mercury.

- Transiting retrograde Pluto in natal fourth house, trine progressed retrograde Mercury and tertiary Sun.
- Transiting Jupiter, at critical degree, in tertiary eighth house, quincunx natal Mercury, square tertiary Sun, semisquare the natal fourth cusp.
- Transiting Venus conjunct natal sixth cusp of health, opposition progressed Mercury, sextile natal and progressed Mars, trine tertiary Sun.
- Transiting Neptune in natal sixth quincunx natal Ascendant and Sun, sextile tertiary Sun.
- Transiting Moon at 18 Leo 00 in natal third house and tertiary sixth conjunct tertiary Pluto; semisquare natal and progressed Uranus and natal Fortuna; semisextile natal Point of Greatest Danger, progressed Part of Peril, and natal fourth cusp; sextile tertiary Neptune.

Although Jay survived this experience, he will always need to be extra careful in his travels, especially in foreign countries.

Chapter 16

Hit by Train

This young woman, age 15, was riding in a car with three friends. They stopped at a railroad crossing to let a train pass. As soon as the train cleared the crossing, the driver of the car sped out, only to be hit by another train coming from the opposite direction.

The event occurred April 15, 1951 at approximately 8:00 pm, latitude 42 North. The other three people were hurt badly, while the young woman suffered a concussion that caused a loss of memory and affected her motor skills; she had to relearn many things such as walking.

In her natal chart we find Saturn (trains) at the same degree as the lunar Nodes. It rules her fourth house and co-rules the fifth of pleasure. On the third cusp is the travel sign of Sagittarius with its ruler, Jupiter, strong in its own sign, straddling that cusp.

Jupiter is the fulcrum of a mutable T-cross but it is sextile the Ascendant (a saver), and semisextile the Sun (a saver). However, it is square the Moon-Neptune conjunction in the eleventh house of friends and square Mars (the head) in the fifth of friends. The latter is conjunct the Point of Greatest Danger and is widely conjunct Saturn.

Retrograde Mercury (youth and transportation) is in the fourth house, semisquare Jupiter and square Uranus, its dispositor.

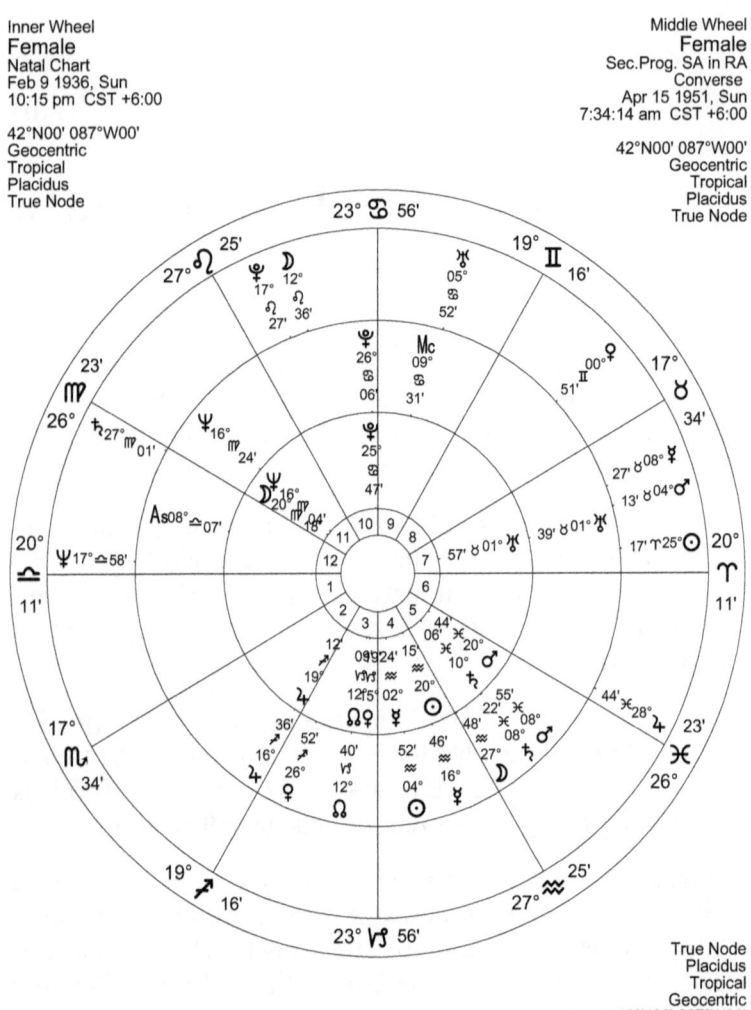

The functioning Moon, afflicted by its conjunction to Neptune, opposes the Mars (danger)-Saturn grouping and is square Jupiter.

Venus, ruling the Ascendant and square it, is in the third of short trips in violent Capricorn, trine the Moon (a saver) and Fortuna (a saver). It is also trine Neptune, sextile Mars, and opposition elevated, retrograde Pluto.

The Point of Accident is in the twelfth house (hidden things) square Venus and trine Part of Death, while Peril is exactly semisextile Pluto and opposition the Sun.

Part of Fatality rises in the map at the degree of the lunar Nodes, sextile Venus, square the Sun and exactly trine Saturn.

Fixed Stars
- Mercury conjunct Geidi (nature of Venus and Mars).
- Uranus conjunct Sharatan (nature of Mars and Saturn).
- Moon conjunct Denebolo (nature of Saturn and Venus).
- Sun conjunct Nashira (nature of Saturn and Jupiter).

Primary Directions
- Venus at 0 Aquarius 18, semisquare Point of Greatest Danger.
- Mercury at 17 Aquarius 23, trine natal Part of Death.
- Sun at 5 Pisces 14, sesquisquare natal Ascendant.
- Saturn at 25 Pisces 00, trine natal Pluto, quincunx natal Part of Peril.
- Mars at 5 Aries 43, semisquare natal Fortuna.
- Uranus at 16 Taurus 54, trine natal Neptune.
- Pluto at 10 Leo 47, square natal Part of Fatality, quincunx natal Saturn, at same degree as lunar Nodes.
- Neptune at 1 Libra 03, quincunx natal Uranus.
- Moon at 5 Libra 14, sesquisquare natal Sun and natal Fortuna.

- Part of Catastrophe at 16 Capricorn 3, trine natal Neptune.
- Part of Peril at 10 Virgo 31, at degree of the Nodes, sextile natal Part of Fatality, opposition natal Saturn.
- Fortuna at 5 Gemini 13, sesquisquare natal Ascendant.

Converse Directions

- Converse Jupiter at 4 Sagittarius 09, critical degree.
- Converse Venus at 0 Capricorn 22, critical degree.
- Converse Mercury at 17 Capricorn 27, trine natal Neptune.
- Converse Sun at 5 Aquarius 10, sesquisquare natal Moon, semisquare natal Mars.
- Converse Saturn at 25 Aquarius 04, opposition natal Part of Peril, quincunx natal Pluto.
- Converse Uranus at 16 Aries 58, quincunx natal Neptune.
- Converse Pluto at 10 Cancer 51 at degree of lunar Nodes, trine natal Saturn, semisquare natal Pluto.
- Converse Neptune at 1 Virgo 07, trine natal Uranus.
- Converse Part of Death at 2 Gemini 31, trine natal Mercury.
- Converse Part of Fatality at 25 Libra 03, square natal Pluto, sextile natal Part of Peril.
- Converse Part of Catastrophe at 16 Sagittarius 57, square natal Neptune.
- Converse Fortuna at 5 Taurus 17, semisquare natal Mars.

Tertiary Directions

- Tertiary retrograde Saturn, ruler of tertiary eighth and ninth houses, in the eleventh house of friends, opposition tertiary and natal Neptune, exactly conjunct natal Mars, square natal and tertiary Jupiter.
- Tertiary Venus conjunct natal and tertiary Neptune and natal Moon, opposition natal and tertiary Saturn and Mars, square natal and tertiary Jupiter. Thus there is a mutable T-cross in the tertiary, backing up the one in the natal chart.
- Tertiary Uranus, retrograde and critical, in the tertiary

twelfth house, square tertiary Mars.
- Mars in the tertiary third house opposition natal Sun and tertiary Moon, ruler of the tertiary third.
- Tertiary Mercury trine natal Mercury, tertiary Sun opposition natal Saturn and square tertiary Ascendant.
- Tertiary Part of Catastrophe straddling tertiary third cusp, conjunct natal and tertiary Pluto.
- Part of Peril conjunct tertiary Ascendant.
- Tertiary Part of Death conjunct natal and tertiary Uranus, square natal Mercury, trine tertiary Mercury and Part of Fatality, square tertiary Venus.

Preceding Eclipses
- March 18, 1950, annular solar eclipse at 27 Pisces 26, conjunct natal sixth cusp of health.
- April 2, 1950, total lunar eclipse at 12 Libra 32, conjunct natal Point of Accident in natal twelfth house.
- September 12, 1950, total solar eclipse at 18 Virgo 48, conjunct natal Neptune, opposition natal Mars and the Point of Greatest Danger.
- September 26, 1950, total lunar eclipse at 2 Aries 26 trine natal Mercury.
- March 7, 1951, annular solar eclipse at 16 Pisces 28 opposition natal Neptune, conjunct the Point of Greatest Danger.

Secondary Progressions
- Progressed Ascendant opposition natal Uranus, square natal Neptune.
- Progressed Sun, at midpoint of natal Sun and Mars, sesquisquare natal Fortuna.
- Progressed Mars semisextile progressed Uranus, square progressed Part of Death and third and ninth cusps.
- Progressed Saturn conjunct progressed fifth cusp, quincunx Point of Accident.

- Progressed Moon at 0 Aries 15 at a critcal degree.
- Progressed eighth cusp at 29 degrees, conjunct the Pleiades, giving something to cry about.

Transits
- Transiting Sun opposition natal Ascendant; square natal, progressed, and tertiary Pluto; square tertiary third cusp and Part of Catastrophe.
- Transiting Mars conjunct natal, progressed and tertiary Uranus; square natal Mercury and tertiary Moon; conjunct tertiary Part of Death; opposition progressed Ascendant, sextile progressed Sun; quincunx tertiary Mercury.
- Transiting retrograde Mercury conjunct tertiary Uranus; semisextile tertiary Ascendant; sextile natal and progressed Saturn and progressed Sun; square tertiary Mars.
- Transiting Venus trine natal Mercury at degree of tertiary lunar Nodes, quincunx natal Part of Catastrophe, sextile tertiary Sun, quincunx tertiary Moon.
- Transiting retrograde Pluto opposition Point of Greatest Danger and natal Sun; semisextile natal, progressed, and tertiary Neptune; sextile natal Ascendant; at same degree as the critical transiting lunar Nodes; sesquisquare tertiary Mercury; sextile natal Part of Death.
- Transiting retrograde Saturn, sextile tertiary Part of Catastrophe and third cusp, conjunct natal twelfth cusp.
- Transiting retrograde Neptune semisextile natal, progressed, and tertiary Neptune; trine natal Part of Death.
- Transiting Jupiter conjunct natal sixth cusp; trine natal, progressed, and tertiary Pluto and tertiary Part of Catastrophe.
- Transiting Moon quincunx natal and progressed Saturn, at same degree as natal lunar Nodes, conjunct tertiary Mars in tertiary third house.

Chapter 17

Shattered Foot

This young man was driving a motorcyle through a shopping center parking lot. Suddenly a car came speeding toward him, and to avoid being hit, he swerved, his right foot hitting the curbstone. The foot was smashed between the cycle and the curbstone, and at first they spoke of amputation, but that drastic surgery was avoided. Later, he had a bone graft.

The only planet in a violent sign in this chart is Jupiter in Aries, ruling the intercepted sixth house of work and health. It is in the eleventh house of hopes and wishes for the future, in opposition to a critical Moon, which in turn is besieged by Saturn and Neptune.

The Part of Peril is on the Ascendant (Saturn ruling the eighth always will do this), also critical, and thus the physical body is critical, or threatened, from birth.

In the first house is chaotic Uranus, also at a critical degree, as the fulcrum of a cardinal cross, with Jupiter at one end and the Moon-Neptune conjunction at the other.

Saturn (the teacher), ruling the public seventh house and the eighth of surgery, is exalted in the fourth, square the Ascendant.

Venus, ruler of the twelfth of hospitals and sorrows, is at the same degree as the lunar Nodes in the fourth house, as is the Sun, ruler of the travel third house.

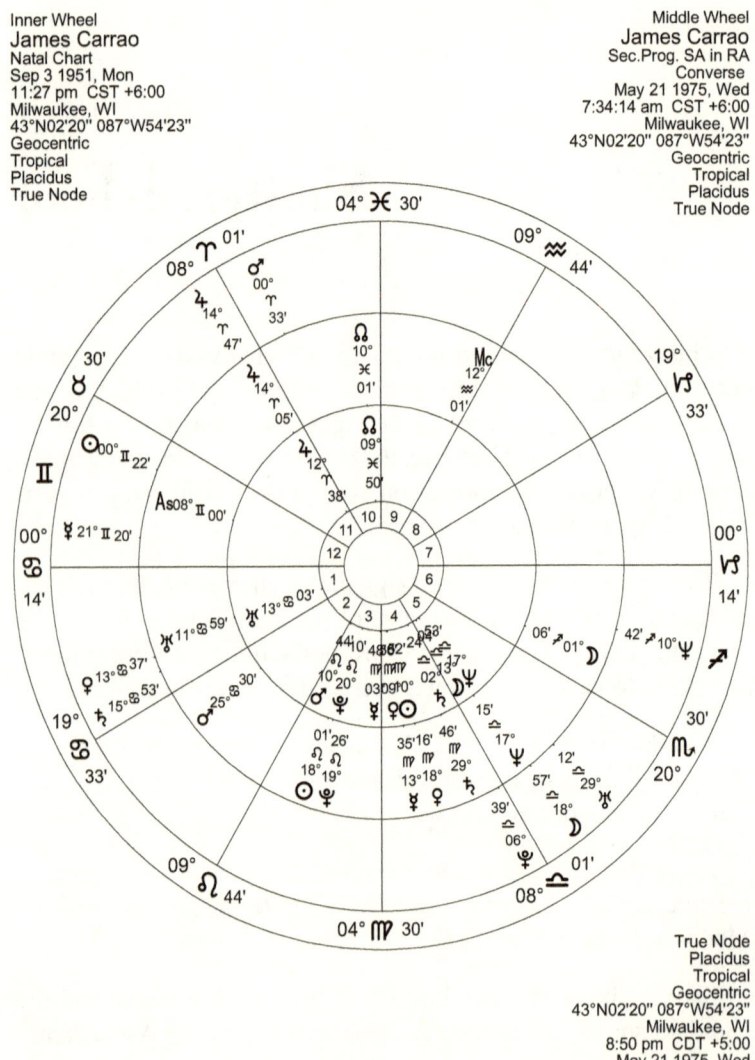

Mars is trine Jupiter and semisextile the Sun from an exact conjunction to the third house cusp. In the third is Pluto close to Mars and void of course, both ruling the sixth of health and work. Also in the third is retrograde Mercury, dignified by rulership and by house position, conjunct the fourth cusp and ruling it, and semisextile Fortuna and trine Part of Catastrophe.

The sixth and twelfth cusps are critical at 21 degrees of fixed signs, bringing crises and activities concerning health and hospital matters.

The Point of Accident is critical, in semisquare aspect to the South Node, Venus, and the Sun, while the Point of Greatest Danger is semisquare Uranus.

The afflictions in Virgo registered in his life as granulomatosis enterocolitis, which destroys the intestines. He had a colostomy performed December 18, 1975 at approximately 9:30 am, at latitude 32N.

Fixed Stars
- Jupiter conjunct Prima Hyadum, nature of Saturn and Mercury.
- Venus conjunct Wasat, nature of Saturn.
- Uranus conjunct Pollux, nature of Mars.
- Mercury and the fifth cusp conjunct the South Ascellus, threatening the eyes, nature of Mars and Sun.

Primary Directions
- Mars at 4 Virgo 04, critical degree.
- Pluto at 13 Virgo 22, semisextile natal Moon.
- Venus at 3 libra 15, sextile natal Fortuna (a saver), quincunx natal Part of Catastrophe.
- Jupiter at 6 Taurus 02, trine Point of Greatest Danger.
- Sun at 3 libra 56, sextile natal Fortuna (a saver), quincunx natal Part of Catastrophe.

- Saturn at 25 libra 38, semisquare natal Sun.
- Moon at 6 Scorpio 30, sextie Point of Greatest Danger.
- Part of Death at 0 Scorpio 47, trine natal Ascendant and Part of Peril.

Converse Directions
- Converse Ascendant and Peril at 7 Gemini 20, semisquare natal Part of Fatality.
- Converse Mars at 17 Cancer 26, square natal Neptune.
- Converse Pluto at 26 Cancer 44, critical degree, conjunct Point of Accident.
- Converse Sun at 1 7 Leo 18, semisextile natal Neptune.
- Converse Saturn at 9 Virgo 00, conjunct natal Venus and South Node.
- Converse Mercury at 10 Leo 31, conjunct natal Mars.
- Converse Fortuna at 9 Cancer 54, sextile natal Venus at same degree as lunar Nodes.
- Converse Part of Catastrophe at 9 Aries 41 at same degree as lunar Nodes, quincunx natal Venus.

Tertiary Directions
- Tertiary Ascendant quincunx natal Saturn.
- Tertiary MC-IC square natal and tertiary Neptune.
- Tertiary Jupiter, ruler of tertiary eighth, rises in tertiary first house (a saver), quincunx natal and tertiary Neptune.
- Tertiary Venus, ruler of tertiary Ascendant, at out-of-rope 29 degrees.
- Tertiary Part of Fatality conjunct fourth cusp.
- Tertiary Uranus conjunct natal Uranus, square natal and tertiary Neptune.
- Tertiary eighth cusp at critical degree.
- Tertiary Sun conjunct natal Part of Fatality, square tertiary Part of Catastrophe.
- Tertiary Mars opposition tertiary Ascendant, square natal

- Mars, sextile natal Sun.
- Tertiary Pluto and Mercury conjunct in tertiary fifth house, conjunct natal Pluto and Part of Surgery.
- Tertiary Nodes at same degree as natal Part of Surgery.
- Tertiary Saturn at same degree as natal lunar Nodes, semisextile natal Venus and Sun, sextile natal Mars.
- Tertiary Part of Fortune opposition natal Sun and Venus, quincunx natal Mars and Moon.
- Tertiary Moon trine natal Saturn, semisquare natal fourth cusp, semisextile natal and tertiary Ascendant.

Preceding Eclipses
- June 4, 1974, partial lunar eclipse at 13 Sagittarius 00, quincunx natal Uranus, sextile natal Moon.
- June 20, 1974, total lunar eclipse at 28 Gemini 30 in natal twelfth house of hospitals, sesquisquare natal Moon.
- November 29, 1974, total lunar eclipse at 7 Gemini 00 sextile natal Mars, square natal Venus and lunar Nodes.
- December 13, 1974, partial lunar eclipse at 21 Sagittarius 17 semisextile natal sixth cusp of health, semisquared natal Part of Death.
- May 11, 1975, partial solar eclipse at 19 Taurus 59, conjunct natal twelfth cusp, quincunx natal Neptune.

Secondary Progressions
- Progressed Ascendant, critical, conjunct natal and progressed Uranus, square natal Moon.
- Progressed Mercury semisextile natal and progressed Pluto.
- Progressed Saturn semisextile natal fourth cusp, semisquare natal and progressed Pluto.
- Progressed Sun semisextile natal Mercury (a saver), quincunx natal Part of Catastrophe.
- Progressed Venus semisextile natal Mars.

- Progressed MC-IC and third and ninth travel cusps at 29 degrees.
- Progressed Moon at 17 Leo 06, semisquare natal Saturn.
- May Part of Fortune semisquare natal Jupiter.

Transits
- Transiting Sun at 29 Taurus, giving something to cry about, square progressed third and ninth cusps, trine progressed fourth cusp, sextile tertiary Venus.
- Transiting Mercury sextile natal, progressed, and tertiary Pluto, square progressed Mercury.
- Transiting Venus conjunct natal, progressed, and tertiary Uranus; quincunx natal eighth house of surgery; trine tertiary Neptune.
- Transiting Saturn conjunct natal, progressed, and tertiary Uranus; sextile progressed Part of Surgery, square progressed Jupiter.
- Transiting retrograde Pluto semisextile Point of Danger; semisquare natal, progressed and tertiary Pluto; semisextile tertiary Part of Death and Mars; conjunct natal Part of Death.
- Transiting retrograde Uranus at 29 degrees, semisextile progressed fourth cusp, square tertiary Venus, sextile progressed third cusp.
- Transiting retrograde Neptune quincunx natal, progressed, and tertiary Uranus; square natal Sun and tertiary Fortuna; trine natal Mars and third cusp and progressed Jupiter.
- Transiting Mars at 20 degrees conjunct progressed MC, quincunx progressed third cusp.
- Transiting Jupiter conjunct natal Jupiter (Jupiter return, a saver), semisextile tertiary Jupiter (a saver).
- Transiting South Node conjunct tertiary Moon.
- Transiting Moon conjunct natal, progressed, and tertiary Neptune; sextile natal, progressed, and tertiary Pluto; semisquare natal Mercury; square tertiary MC-IC and Part of Fatality.

Chapter 18

Train Crash

For many years this gentleman commuted to and from his work via the El in Chicago and every day he sat in the last car of the train. On November 24, 1936, as he approached the train, he noticed a small fire on one of the tracks and after some deliberation he decided to remain where he was and watch the activity of the men putting out the fire. Because of this decision, the last car was filled when he went aboard the El, so he had to move forward to another car.

The following morning the newspaper headlines read, "Chicago EL Crash Kills 8 and Injures 60."

At 6:20 pm, the Northshore line's steel train had sheared through the rear car of the wooden Evanston train on which this gentleman was riding. Because he had no need of the drastic experience of injury or death and so decided to remain and watch the fire, thus having to vary his normal routine by sitting in another car on the train, he experienced only a shaking-up and mental and emotional trauma.

In his natal chart we find the lunar Nodes at the out-of-rope twenty-ninth degree, but there are no planets at this same degree and there are no critical degrees.

The only two planets in violent signs are the third-house Mercury in Capricorn and the twelfth-house Moon in Scorpio.

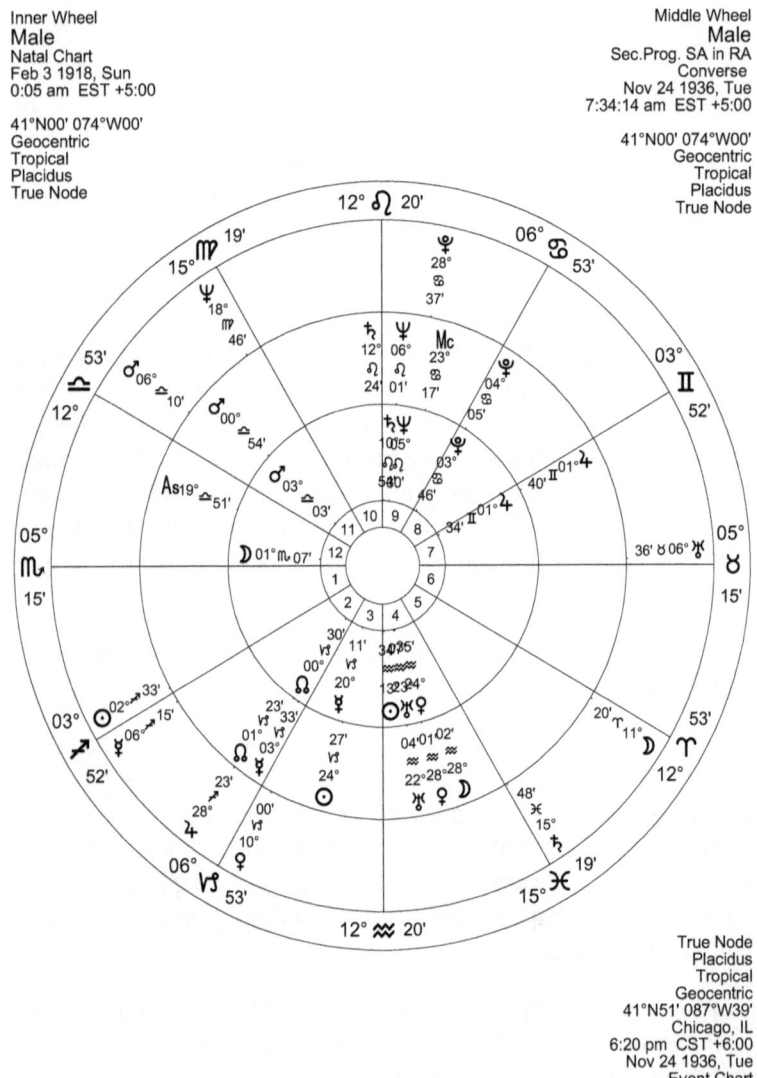

Moon, ruler of the ninth travel house, detrimented, conjunct Ascendant from the twelfth house, fulcrum of a fixed T-cross with the Sun-Neptune opposition.

Retrograde Neptune, ruler of the third of short-distance travel, opposition fourth-house Sun.

Mercury in the third house of short trips, strong by house position; only aspects are a semisextile to Venus and Uranus in the fourth house.

Jupiter (greater benefic) exactly quincunx Moon, part of an air grand trine with Mars, ruler of the sixth house of health, and Sun, ruler of the tenth (a saver).

Retrograde Venus (lesser benefic) in the fourth house, just past the conjunction to a dignified Uranus, void of course.

Retrograde Pluto (Ascendant ruler) in the eighth, trine Ascendant, square Mars, square third-house Mercury by sign only.

Part of Catastrophe rises in exact quincunx to Part of Peril in the sixth of work.

Primary Directions
- Ascendant at 23 Scorpio 30, square natal Uranus.
- Jupiter at 20 Gemini 06, quincunx natal Mercury, semisquare natal Pluto.
- Pluto at 22 Cancer 18, conjunct natal Fortuna.
- Neptune at 24 Leo 01, opposition natal Venus.
- Fortuna at 10 Leo 49, conjunct natal Saturn.
- Part of Peril at 2 Taurus 50, conjunct natal Part of Fatality.
- Part of Death at 25 Gemini 53, semisquare natal Saturn.

The danger was real but because most of the aspects were minor, the threat and pressure were not as personal; they related more to his involvement with others.

Converse Directions
- Converse Ascendant at 16 Libra 28, sesquisquare natal Jupiter.
- Converse Mercury at 1 Capricorn 41, sextile natal Moon, quincunx natal Jupiter.
- Converse Neptune at 16 Cancer 59, semisquare natal Jupiter. (All aspects to Jupiter set off his grand trine—a saver.)
- Converse Mars at 14 Virgo 33, sextile natal Part of Catastrophe, quincunx natal Part of Peril.
- Converse Fortuna at 3 Cancer 47, conjunct natal Pluto.
- Converse Part of Catastrophe at 26 Libra 04, critical degree.
- Part of Fatality at 13 Aries 47, critical degree.
- Part of Peril at 25 Pisces 48, sesquisquare natal Saturn.

Tertiary Directions
- Tertiary Ascendant sextile tertiary Mercury, opposition Part of Peril Uranus (then void of course—not much activity).
- Tertiary Sun conjunct fixed star Vindemiatrix of the nature of Saturn and Mercury (trains and travel).
- Tertiary Moon, ruler of tertiary Ascendant, sextile tertiary Pluto and natal ninth cusp, conjunct natal Point of Greatest Danger.
- Tertiary Jupiter exalted, conjunct Pluto in the behind-the-scenes twelfth house (the train was hit from behind), trine natal Part of Fatality, square natal Part of Peril.
- Tertiary Mars sextile natal Mars, semisextile natal Moon and Ascendant, quincunx natal and tertiary Pluto and Jupiter, trine natal and progressed Neptune, ruler of the critical tertiary MC.
- Tertiary Saturn exactly opposition natal Venus and eighth-house tertiary Uranus, quincunx Ascendant and Part of Peril Saturn.
- Tertiary Venus conjunct tertiary Mercury in tertiary third house of travel. They make no aspect to the natal chart but

are quincunx tertiary Uranus, forming a yod with the tertiary Ascendant and Part of Peril Saturn, and square tertiary Part of Fortune.
- Tertiary IC, at critical degree, trine natal Sun (a saver).

Preceding Eclipses
- January 8, 1936, total lunar eclipse at 17 Cancer 19 in natal ninth house, semisquare natal and progressed Jupiter.
- June 19, 1936, total solar eclipse at 27 Gemini 44 in natal eighth house, semisquare natal Saturn and MC.
- July 4, 1936, partial lunar eclipse at 12 Capricorn 31 in natal third house, semisextile natal Sun and progressed Venus, sextile natal Part of Catastrophe, square natal Part of Peril.

Secondary Progressions
- Progressed Ascendant semisquare natal Mars, sesquisquare natal and progressed Pluto.
- Progressed Mars, quincunx progressed Sun, trine progressed Jupiter, semisextile natal Moon.
- Progressed Sun trine natal Moon, square natal Jupiter.
- Progressed Fortuna sesquisquare natal Saturn.
- Progressed Venus square natal Part of Catastrophe, sextile natal Part of Peril.
- Progressed Moon semisextile progressed Saturn, sesquisquare natal and progressed Uranus.
- Progressed Part of Catastrophe opposition progressed Jupiter.
- Progressed Part of Death semisextile progressed Jupiter.
- Progressed Saturn had been critical for a number of years.

Transits
- Transiting Sun conjunct progressed Part of Catastrophe, quincunx natal Part of Fatality and progressed Part of Peril,

opposition natal and progressed Jupiter, sextile natal and progressed Mars, conjunct tertiary Mars.
- Transiting Mercury semisquare natal Mercury; opposition natal and progressed Jupiter, quincunx natal, progressed, and tertiary Pluto; trines natal, progressed, and tertiary Neptune; square natal Point of Greatest Danger.
- Transiting Jupiter conjunct progressed North Node, quincunx tertiary Ascendant and Part of Peril Saturn, semisextile tertiary Part of Peril Uranus, square tertiary Mercury, conjunct tertiary sixth cusp.
- Transiting Venus in natal third house quincunxes natal, progressed, and tertiary Neptune and natal and progressed Saturn; square tertiary Sun; opposition progressed Moon.
- Transiting Saturn trine natal Part of Catastrophe, semisextiles natal Part of Peril and Mercury, square natal Point of Accident, conjunct natal fifth cusp, trine tertiary Jupiter.
- Transiting retrograde Uranus opposition natal Ascendant, square natal and progressed Saturn.
- Transiting retrograde Pluto sesquisquares natal Part of Catastrophe, at same degree as the progressed lunar Nodes, conjunct tertiary Ascendant and Part of Peril Saturn, opposition Part of Peril Uranus, quincunx tertiary Mercury.
- Transiting Neptune quincunx natal Venus and Uranus, square progressed Part of Fatality, semisquare natal and progressed Neptune, sextile progressed Ascendant, semisquare natal Ascendant.
- Transiting Mars conjunct natal and progressed Mars; semisextile tertiary Moon; sextile natal, progressed and tertiary Neptune.
- Transiting lunar Nodes at same degree as tertiary Mercury.
- Transiting Moon trine progressed Saturn; semisquare natal and progressed Uranus, natal Venus and tertiary Uranus; trine Point of Accident.

Chapter 19

Third-degree Burns

At three years of age, on February 4, 1947, at approximately 10:30 am, this child was trying to light candles on her father's birthday cake. He was coming home from an out-of-town trip, and her mother had left the room for a moment. The child's robe caught on fire and had spread to her hair by the time her mother, hearing the screams, came running. Her mother grabbed a tea towel and smothered the flames on the child's head, then proceeded to beat out the rest of the fire. Because of the heavy cotton robe and nightgown that the child was wearing, the flames did not spread as fast as they might have, and this saved her. However, she suffered third-degree burns from the waist down, including her legs, and spent the next three and a half months in the hospital. She had skin grafts and plastic surgery.

In this chart we find Mercury, ruler of the Ascendant and MC, strong in its own sign and exactly conjunct the MC. It is conjunct Uranus and Saturn as part of a minor stellium in Gemini, posited in the tenth house, and widely square Mars, planet of fire.

Mars opposes the Ascendant, is sextile the Sun and square Saturn, as well as the entire Gemini grouping. It is also trine Jupiter, quincunx Fortuna in the twelfth house, and widely opposition Neptune.

Jupiter, co-ruler of 29-degree eighth house cusp and fourth of the home, exalted, is square the Moon.

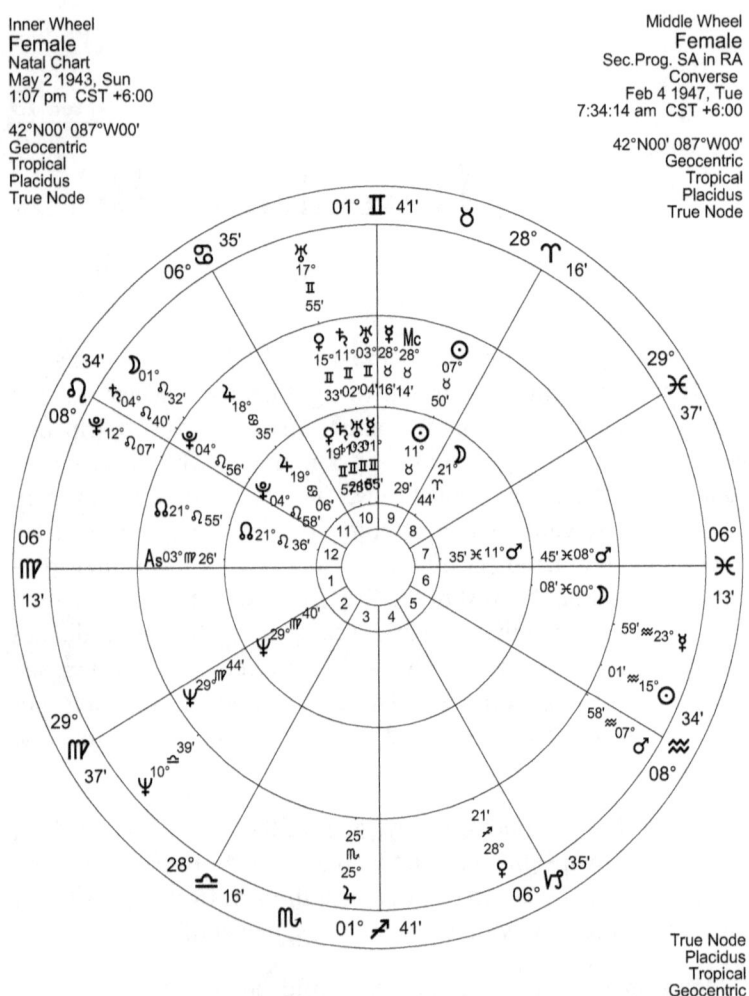

The eighth-house Moon in the fire sign Aries is at the same degree as the lunar Nodes, sesquisquare Part of Surgery and opposition the Point of Accident.

The Part of Catastrophe is conjunct the rising retrograde Neptune, at the out-of-rope 29 degrees, the latter straddling the second cusp, opposing the eighth.

Pluto in the fire sign Leo is square the Sun and semisquare Venus. The Parts of Fatality, Death, and Peril Jupiter, as well as the Parts of Accident and Greatest Danger, are all in the second house, all in the cardinal Venus (beauty, skin)-ruled sign of Libra. Part of Peril Jupiter and the Point of Greatest Danger are at critical degrees.

In the fourth house, which has the fire sign Sagittarius on the cusp, we find the Part of Surgery exactly square the Ascendant and Part of Peril Neptune, the latter in trine aspect to the Moon.

The Sun, ruler of the twelfth of hospitals, is square Fortuna, semisextile Saturn, and sextile Jupiter (a saver).

Fixed Stars
- Moon conjunct Baten Kaitos (nature of Saturn).
- Uranus conjunct Prima Hyadum (nature of Saturn and Mercury).
- Venus conjunct Capella (nature of Mars and Mercury).

Primary Directions
- Neptune at 3 libra 19, trine natal Uranus.
- Mars at 15 Pisces 11, quincunx natal Fortuna.
- Sun at 15 Taurus 05, square natal Fortuna.
- Midheaven at 4 Gemini 36, critical degree, semisquare natal Jupiter.
- Mercury at 5 Gemini 31, trine natal Part of Fatality, opposition natal Part of Surgery.

- Saturn at 15 Gemini 03, sextile natal Fortuna.
- Venus at 23 Gemini 33, opposition natal Part of Peril Neptune.
- Jupiter at 22 Cancer 40, square Point of Accident.
- Pluto at 8 Leo 35, conjunct natal twelfth cusp, sesquisquare natal Part of Peril Neptune.
- Fortuna at 19 Leo 30, sextile natal Venus and semisextile natal Jupiter (savers).
- Part of Catastrophe at 0 libra 02, critical degree, semisquare natal Fortuna.
- Part of Death and Part of Peril Jupiter at 16 libra 00, sesquisquare natal Mercury, semisquare natal fourth cusp.
- Part of Peril Neptune at 27 Sagittarius 32, square natal Part of Catastrophe.

Converse Directions

- Converse Neptune at 26 Virgo 27, semisextile Point of Greatest Danger, sesquisquare natal Sun.
- Converse Mars at 7 Pisces 59, semisquare Point of Accident.
- Converse Moon at 18 Aries 07, semisquare natal Uranus.
- Converse MC at 27 Taurus 24, trine natal Part of Catastrophe.
- Converse Mercury at 28 Taurus 19, sesquisquare natal Part of Peril Jupiter.
- Converse Jupiter at 15 Cancer 28, semisextile natal Fortuna (a saver).
- Converse Pluto at 1 Leo 18, sextile natal Mercury.
- Converse Fortuna at 12 Leo 18, sextile natal Part of Death.
- Converse Part of Catastrophe at 23 Virgo 50, square natal Part of Peril Neptune.
- Converse Part of Surgery at 1 Sagittarius 55, opposition natal Mercury.

Tertiary Directions
- Tertiary Venus (ruler of tertiary Ascendant and tertiary eighth house, strong in its own sign) in tertiary eighth house quincunx natal Part of Death, sesquisquare tertiary and natal Neptune.
- Tertiary Saturn (ruler of tertiary fourth house of home) critical and conjunct tertiary ninth house cusp (also critical), square natal Mars and Ascendant.
- Tertiary Mars, detrimented and void of course, sextile natal Neptune.
- Tertiary Sun conjunct natal Venus (a saver), but tertiary Jupiter, although exalted, is at a critical degree; semisextile natal and tertiary Uranus, natal MC and Mercury and tertiary Saturn; opposition natal Part of Peril Neptune.
- Tertiary Uranus in tertiary eighth house of surgery, conjunct natal Mercury, square tertiary Part of Death.
- Tertiary Moon conjunct natal Saturn, trine tertiary Ascendant (a saver); semisextile tertiary MC (line of destiny); square tertiary Part of Peril, Part of Catastrophe, and Part of Fatality.
- Tertiary Pluto semisextile natal Ascendant, sextile tertiary Ascendant.
- Tertiary retrograde Mercury (strong in its own sign, like the natal map), conjunct tertiary Sun, square natal and tertiary Neptune, at same degree as critical natal lunar Nodes, sextile natal Moon, opposition natal Part of Peril Neptune, square tertiary Part of Fatality and Fortuna.
- The Parts of Death, Fatality, Peril, and Catastrophe are grouped in the same sign, Virgo, all disposited by the tertiary Mercury.

Preceding Eclipses
- May 30, 1946, solar eclipse at 8 Gemini 49, conjunct natal and progressed Saturn, semisquare natal Moon.
- June 14, 1946, lunar eclipse at 22 Sagittarius 54, opposition

natal Venus, trine natal Moon, sextile Point of Accident.
- June 29, 1946, partial solar eclipse at 6 Cancer 49, conjunct natal eleventh cusp of circumstances beyond our control, square Part of Fatality, quincunx natal and progressed Part of Surgery.
- November 23, 1946, partial solar eclipse at 0 Sagittarius 49 opposition natal and progressed Mercury and natal and progressed Uranus, conjunct natal fourth cusp of the home.
- December 8, 1946, total lunar eclipse at 15 Gemini 54, conjunct natal Venus, sextile natal Fortuna, square natal and progressed Mars.

Secondary Progressions
- Progressed Mercury conjunct natal and progressed Uranus.
- Progressed fourth cusp at critical degree, sesquisquare natal and progressed Jupiter.
- Progressed Pluto semisextile natal Ascendant and natal Part of Fatality.
- Progressed Venus opposition progressed Part of Peril Neptune.
- Progressed Sun sesquisquare natal and progressed Neptune.

These were the only progressions in force, and this condition helped to save her.

Transits
- Transiting Sun conjunct natal and progressed Mars, quincunx natal Part of Peril Jupiter, square natal and progressed Saturn, opposition tertiary Part of Catastrophe, conjunct tertiary sixth cusp of health, sesquisquare tertiary Mars.
- Transiting Mars at out-of-rope 29 degrees quincunx natal, progressed, and tertiary Neptune; quincunx tertiary Mars.
- Transiting Uranus at critical degree conjunct tertiary Sun.

Secondary Progressions

- Transiting retrograde Saturn in fire sign Leo conjunct natal and progressed Pluto; semisextile natal and progressed Mercury and natal, progressed, and tertiary Uranus; semisquare tertiary Part of Catastrophe; semisextile tertiary Part of Death.
- Transiting retrograde Neptune trine natal and progressed Saturn, quincunx natal Mars, in tertiary Ascendant, quincunx tertiary Venus, trine tertiary Moon.
- Transiting retrograde Mercury at degree of tertiary lunar Nodes; square natal and progressed Venus, tertiary Sun and Mercury; opposition tertiary Part of Fatality and tertiary Fortuna.
- Transiting Jupiter sextile natal, progressed, and tertiary Neptune; semisquare natal Part of Death; trine tertiary Mars and natal eighth cusp.
- Transiting Venus at 29 degrees trine natal and progressed Neptune, opposition tertiary Mars, sextile natal eighth cusp.
- Transiting Moon square natal Sun and tertiary Venus, quincunx natal Mars, sextile tertiary Moon.

Chapter 20

Motorcycle Accident

This man's motorcycle hit some loose gravel as he was driving home from work at 4:00 pm on June 13, 1973, at latitude 40N. Losing control, he flipped over the cycle and, on landing, broke his clavicle (collar bone).

A couple of weeks later he developed a bad staph infection that could not be isolated. Drugs did nothing to clear up the infection, which continued to worsen. As a last resort, the doctor decided to try a new, dangerous drug. It was a cure or kill decision that finally cleared up the infection.

In the fourth house we find retrograde Uranus, ruler of the travel third house, in the violent sign of Aries, square the eighth-house (surgery) Pluto.

Neptune (drugs), co-ruler of intercepted Pisces in the third travel house, is in the ninth, intercepted and conjunct critical Mercury (clavicle), both of them square the twelfth house (hospital) Moon and quincunx critical Fortuna in the third. (Interceptions indicate delayed activity, and thus the event happened later in the life cycle.) Mars is also in the ninth, square the rising retrograde Saturn of falls.

The Sagittarius (blood) Ascendant is ruled by a detrimented Jupiter in the sixth of health (he has had many health problems during his lifetime). It closely opposes the Ascendant and Moon,

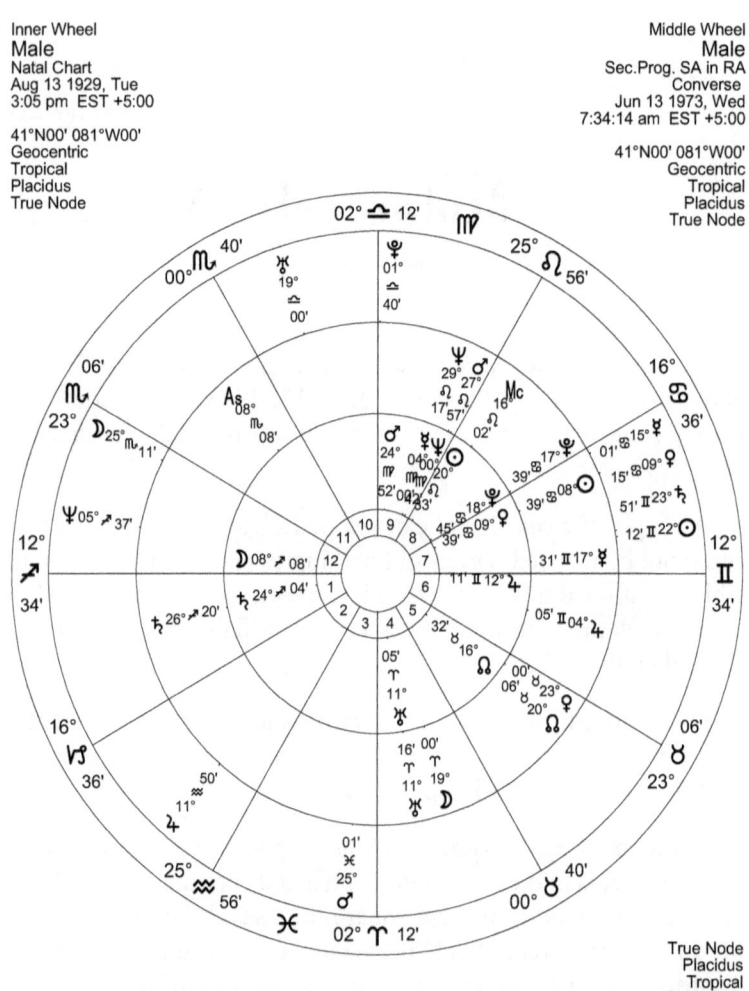

widely opposes rising Saturn, and is widely square Mars, thus forming a mutable T-cross.

Venus, the lesser benefic, is square the fourth-house Uranus (44 years is four times the degree of the latter).

The life-giving Sun, ruler of the ninth, is in the eighth of surgery, dignified in the sign of the heart (he now has heart problems), trine Saturn and widely trine Uranus, forming a wide grand trine in fire (a saver).

Fixed Stars
- Sun conjunct Algenubi (nature of Saturn and Mars).
- Mars conjunct Copula (nature of Saturn and Mars).
- Moon conjunct Han (nature of Saturn and Venus).
- Saturn conjunct Aculeus (nature of Mars and Moon).
- Third cusp conjunct Caput Algol (nature of Saturn and Jupiter).

Primary Directions
- Ascendant at 26 Capricorn 23, critical degree.
- Uranus at 23 Taurus 18, conjunct natal sixth cusp of work and health and Caput Algol.
- Pluto at 1 Virgo 54, sesquisquare natal Part of Fatality.
- Sun at 3 libra 45, conjunct natal Midheaven.
- Neptune at 13 libra 54, critical degree, sextile natal Ascendant.
- Part of Fatality at 29 Taurus 55, out-of-rope 29 degrees, conjunct the Pleiades, giving something to cry about.
- Part of Catastrophe at 16 Virgo 56, same degree as lunar Nodes, quincunx natal Part of Fatality.

Converse Directions
- Converse Uranus at 27 Aquarius 54, sesquisquare natal Jupiter.
- Converse Jupiter at 18 Aries 57, square natal Pluto.

- Converse Mercury at 20 Cancer 48, semisextile natal Sun (a saver).
- Converse Mars at 11 Leo 41, trine natal Uranus.
- Converse Moon at 24 Libra 54, semisextile natal Mars, sextile natal Saturn.
- Converse Fortuna at 17 Aquarius 28, trine natal Mercury (a saver).
- Converse Part of Death at 09 Gemini 18, semisextile natal Venus.
- Converse Part of Catastrophe at 20 Gemini 32, sextile natal Sun.

Tertiary Directions
- Tertiary Ascendant conjunct natal Sun in natal eighth house.
- Tertiary Venus opposition tertiary Ascendant and natal Sun from tertiary sixth house of health, quincunx natal and tertiary Pluto.
- Tertiary Saturn (strong in its own sign and conjunct tertiary sixth cusp, which it rules) square tertiary Moon, trine natal Mars, opposition tertiary Mars.
- Tertiary Moon in tertiary ninth house square tertiary Mars, fulcrum of cardinal T-cross in the tertiary chart.
- Tertiary Uranus in tertiary ninth sextile tertiary Venus, square tertiary Jupiter-Pluto conjunction, square tertiary Saturn, forming another cardinal cross in the tertiary map.
- Tertiary Mars in tertiary twelfth house trine tertiary Sun, the latter posited in the tertiary eighth house.
- Tertiary Mercury in natal ninth of travel, in tertiary eighth house, conjunct tertiary ninth cusp, trine natal Moon.
- Tertiary Jupiter conjunct natal and tertiary Pluto, conjunct natal Venus (a saver), square natal Uranus.
- Tertiary Neptune rises in tertiary chart, conjunct natal Neptune and Mercury and tertiary Part of Catastrophe, quincunx natal Mercury.

- Tertiary fifth and eleventh cusps critical at 17 degrees mutable.

Preceding Eclipses
- January 16, 1972, total solar eclipse at 25 Capricorn 25 trine natal Mars, semisextile natal Saturn.
- January 30, 1972, partial lunar eclipse at 9 Leo 00, critical degree, in natal eighth house, semisquare natal Mars, sesquisquare natal Saturn, trine natal and progressed Uranus.
- July 10, 1972, total solar eclipse at 18 Cancer 37 in natal eighth house, conjunct natal and progressed Pluto, semisquare natal Mercury and progressed Neptune.
- July 26, 1972, partial lunar eclipse at 2 Aquarius 00 opposition natal Part of Catastrophe, quincunx natal and progressed Neptune and natal Mercury and progressed Venus, sextile natal fourth cusp.
- January 4, 1973, partial solar eclipse at 14 Capricorn 08 opposition natal and progressed Pluto at same degree as the progressed lunar Nodes.
- June 15, 1973 (two days after the event), lunar eclipse at 24 Sagittarius 00 (blood) conjunct natal Saturn and square natal Mars (the infection).

Secondary Progressions
- Progressed Ascendant opposition natal Part of Death, square progressed Mars.
- Progressed Venus conjunct natal Neptune.
- Progressed Mercury, quincunx natal sixth cusp, semisextile natal twelfth cusp.
- Progressed Sun semisquare progressed MC, semisextile natal Neptune.
- Progressed Moon at 6 Cancer 00 just past semisquare to natal Moon.
- Progressed Fortuna at 26 libra 24, at critical degree.

Transits

- Transiting Sun-Saturn opposition in opposition to natal and progressed Saturn, quincunx tertiary Saturn, square natal Mars, trine progressed Mars and Mercury, quincunx progressed Ascendant.
- Transiting Venus-transiting South Node conjunction conjunct natal Venus, square natal and progressed Uranus, trine Point of Greatest Danger.
- Transiting Mercury at degree of progressed lunar Nodes between tertiary Jupiter and natal, progressed, and tertiary Pluto.
- Progressed Part of Fatality and tertiary Sun trine progressed MC, sextile progressed fourth cusp, square tertiary Uranus, quincunx tertiary Venus.
- Transiting Pluto (stationary direct) semisextile natal and progressed Neptune and progressed Venus, conjunct progressed Sun, opposition natal Fortuna, semisquare natal South Node and progressed MC.
- Transiting Uranus square natal, progressed, and tertiary Pluto and tertiary Saturn.
- Transiting retrograde Jupiter sextile natal and tertiary Uranus, quincunx tertiary Jupiter, in tertiary sixth house, trine natal and progressed Jupiter (a saver).
- Transiting Mars in natal third house opposition natal Mars, square natal Saturn, quincunx progressed Mars and Mercury, square Point of Accident, sextile tertiary Moon, trine tertiary Mars.
- Transiting Moon at 25 Scorpio in natal twelfth and tertiary fourth; sextile natal Mars; semisextile natal and progressed Saturn and progressed Mars, Mercury, and Fortuna; trine tertiary Mars; quincunx tertiary Moon, trine tertiary Sun.

Chapter 21

Car Accident

On the afternoon of July 2, 1972, at approximately 2:05 pm at latitude 33N, as Gloria was making a left turn, another car tried to beat the light and hit Gloria's car. Her pelvis was broken in two places, she suffered three cracked ribs, and her upper right arm was deeply cut by broken glass.

In the chart we find Saturn (bones) in violent Aries in the eleventh house of circumstances beyond our control. The Part of Peril is exactly conjunct the Ascendant, and the Point of Accident rises close to the first cusp.

The four-planet stellium in Cancer contains a weak Mars, in its fall, while Mercury, ruler of the Ascendant, is sextile Neptune (hidden things), and besieged by Mars and Pluto.

Venus, ruling the sixth of health and the twelfth of hospitals, is also in the third house, close to the fourth Cusp (home), bringing danger from the right side of the road, near her home base. It is square the twelfth-house Uranus, sextile the Point of Accident, and trine Saturn. The greater benefic, Jupiter, strong in its co-rulership of Pisces, ruling the public seventh house of open enemies, is elevated in the map (a saver) and square the Ascendant and the Point of greatest Danger.

The Moon, ruling the third of travel and in the fourth house, is in mutual reception with the Sun (a saver). Its position in its own

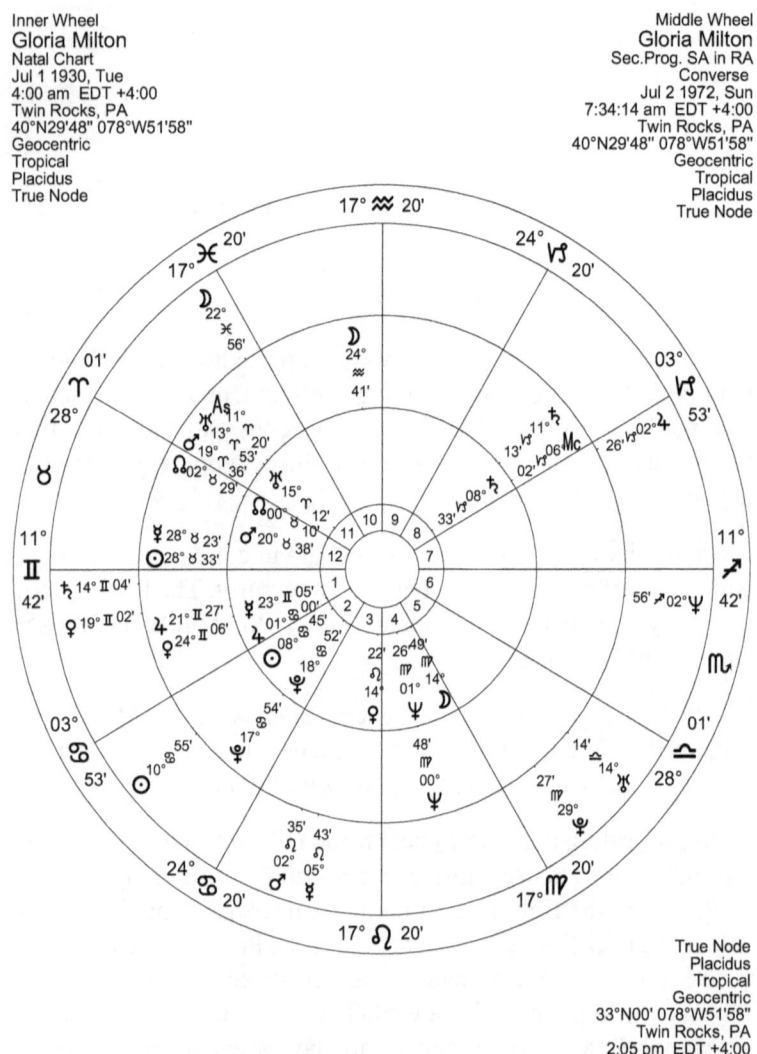

sign puts it in conjunction with the out-of-rope Pluto and Fortuna in the third, and it is almost void of course, its only aspect being a weak semisextile to the Pluto-Fortuna conjunction.

The Ascendant in travel Gemini is square Neptune and semisquare the third cusp.

The fourth cusp is at the midpoint of the Mercury-Neptune sextile, making it an even more sensitive point.

The third and ninth cusps (travel houses) are at the same degree as the lunar Nodes, while the fifth and eleventh cusps are at critical degrees.

Fixed Stars
- Moon between Aljabah (nature of Saturn and Mercury), and Regulus (nature of Mars and Jupiter).
- Jupiter conjunct Sadalmelik (nature of Saturn and Mercury).
- Uranus conjunct Menkar (nature of Saturn).
- South Node conjunct Caput Algol (nature of Saturn and Jupiter).

Primary Directions
- Ascendant and Part of Peril at 14 Cancer 29, semisextile natal Venus (a saver).
- Pluto and Fortuna at 2 Virgo 37, sesquisquare natal Saturn, opposition natal Jupiter.
- Venus at 18 Virgo 29, conjunct natal Neptune, sextile natal Mercury.
- Moon at 0 Libra 52, critical degree.
- Part of Catastrophe at 16 Taurus 13, conjunct natal Uranus.
- Part of Fatality at 16 Aries 51, opposition natal Part of Death, semisquare Point of Greatest Danger.

Converse Directions
- Converse Mars at 12 Gemini 27, sextile natal Part of Catastrophe and square natal Part of Surgery.
- Converse Neptune at 15 Leo 06, semisextile natal Mars.
- Converse Saturn at 13 Pisces 47, conjunct natal Part of Fatality.
- Converse Uranus at 13 Aries 09, critical degree.
- Converse Part of Fatality at 9 Aquarius 47, critical degree.
- Fourth cusp at 13 Cancer 28, critical degree.

Tertiary Directions
- Tertiary Ascendant conjunct natal Moon.
- Tertiary Sun, ruler of tertiary Ascendant, square natal Sun, opposition tertiary Jupiter, co-ruler of and in tertiary eighth house.
- Tertiary Moon opposition tertiary Sun (Full Moon, culmination cycle), square tertiary Part of Peril Jupiter and natal Sun, quincunx natal Jupiter, trine tertiary Pluto, sextile tertiary Mars.
- Tertiary Mercury and Venus opposition natal Saturn and Part of Catastrophe, trine natal Ascendant (a saver) and natal Part of Catastrophe.
- Tertiary retrograde Uranus at critical degree, elevated in tertiary travel ninth house, trine tertiary Neptune, in its fall, square natal Moon and tertiary Ascendant, sextile natal Pluto and Fortuna, quincunx tertiary Part of Peril Neptune.
- Tertiary retrograde Saturn, ruler of tertiary sixth of health, elevated in tenth house, ruling tertiary public seventh house, at out-of-rope 29 degrees, conjunct Pleiades (giving something to cry about), sextile natal Pluto and Fortuna, void of course in the tertiary chart, trine sixth house cusp, sextile to the twelfth cusp.
- Tertiary Mars in tertiary sixth house of health, co-rules tertiary fourth, opposition Pluto, semisextile natal Jupiter.
- Tertiary Neptune (ruler of tertiary eighth house) rises in ter-

tiary chart, quincunx tertiary Fortuna, opposition tertiary Ascendant from the sixth house side.

Preceding Eclipses
- July 22, 1971, partial solar eclipse at 28 Cancer 55 in natal third house, conjunct natal Fortuna and natal and progressed Pluto, quincunx progressed Jupiter.
- August 6, 1971, total lunar eclipse at 13 Aquarius 30 in natal ninth house, opposition natal Venus, square natal and progressed Uranus.
- August 20, 1971, partial lunar eclipse at 27 Leo 15 in natal fourth, conjunct natal Moon, sextile natal Ascendant, sesquisquare natal Part of Catastrophe.
- January 4, 1972, partial solar eclipse at 14 Capricorn 08 opposition natal Mars and progressed Part of Peril, semisquare progressed Jupiter, trine natal and progressed Uranus and progressed Part of Catastrophe, square natal and progressed Saturn, trine natal and progressed Neptune.

Secondary Progressions
- Progressed Mercury sextile progressed Ascendant and natal Sun (two savers).
- Progressed Venus at same degree as natal lunar Nodes, semisextile progressed third cusp, which is also at the degree of the natal lunar Nodes and sextile natal third cusp.
- Progressed Ascendant is conjunct natal Sun (a saver).
- Progressed Moon at 15 Scorpio trine natal Mars, quincunx the Point of Greatest Danger.
- Progressed Fortuna just past progressed Sun, trine natal Part of Catastrophe, quincunx natal Part of Surgery.

Transits
- Transiting Sun conjunct natal Sun and progressed Ascendant, semisextile natal Ascendant (a saver), square tertiary Mercury and Venus.

- Transiting Mars conjunct tertiary Pluto, quincunx natal Jupiter, semisquare natal critical fifth cusp and natal and progressed Neptune and Point of Greatest Danger, semisextile tertiary Sun and Part of Peril Jupiter, trine tertiary Moon and Jupiter, opposition tertiary Mars.
- Transiting Mercury semisquare natal and progressed Neptune, quincunx natal Jupiter, semisextile tertiary Sun, trine tertiary Jupiter and Moon.
- Transiting Pluto at out-of-rope 29 degrees sextile natal Fortuna and natal and progressed Pluto, trine tertiary Saturn, quincunx progressed Jupiter.
- Transiting Uranus square progressed Part of Peril and natal Mars; conjunct tertiary Mercury and Venus; sesquisquare progressed Jupiter; opposition natal and progressed Saturn, progressed Part of Surgery, and Part of Fatality; sesquisquare tertiary third cusp.
- Transiting retrograde Neptune sesquisquare natal and progressed Saturn, progressed Part of Surgery and Part of Fatality, and natal Mars; square tertiary Moon and Jupiter; quincunx tertiary Sun; sextiles tertiary Mars and Sun; square natal Jupiter; trine tertiary Pluto.
- Transiting retrograde Jupiter trine natal Jupiter and tertiary Pluto; sesquisquare natal and progressed Uranus; square tertiary Moon, Jupiter, and Sun; sextile tertiary Mars.
- Transiting Saturn in natal first house conjuncts natal Ascendant and Point of Accident, sextile tertiary Part of Catastrophe, semisquare natal and progressed Pluto and natal Fortuna, square natal Part of Surgery and Part of Fatality.
- Transiting retrograde Venus in natal first conjunct Point of Accident, square natal and progressed Neptune, semisextile natal Mercury, square tertiary Part of Peril Neptune.
- Transiting Moon at 23 Pisces conjunct progressed MC, opposition progressed fourth cusp and tertiary Neptune, in tertiary eighth, semisextile tertiary Fortuna (a saver), trine tertiary fourth cusp, quincunx tertiary Ascendant and natal Moon.

Chapter 22

Car Crash

This event happened at latitude 34N on October 19, 1953 at approximately 11:00 pm, as this woman was driving along a newly paved road on which there were no street lights. She had to swerve suddenly in order to avoid being hit by an oncoming car that had lost its power and thus was out of control. This caused her to smash into a parked car.

She suffered a broken wrist and kneecap, head cuts and concussion, internal head injuries, and abrasions of the eyes.

In the chart we find Saturn void of course in the twelfth house of sorrows and hospitals in its fall in violent Capricorn, exactly sextile Part of Death. We also find an elevated retrograde Uranus in violent Capricorn, disposited by the twelfth-house Saturn and exactly quincunx Pluto. The Sun rises in this map (a saver) semisquare Pluto, sextile Neptune, and exactly quincunx Part of Peril (she had a number of other accidents) and the Point of Accident, trine the MC/Part of Catastrophe conjunction, sextile the fourth cusp.

Venus (lesser benefic, Ascendant ruler and sixth-house co-ruler) in the twelfth of hospitals, strong in its sign of exaltation, sextile Uranus, square Pluto.

Neptune (twelfth-house ruler and dispositor of Venus) in the third of travel conjunct fourth cusp, bringing danger on the right

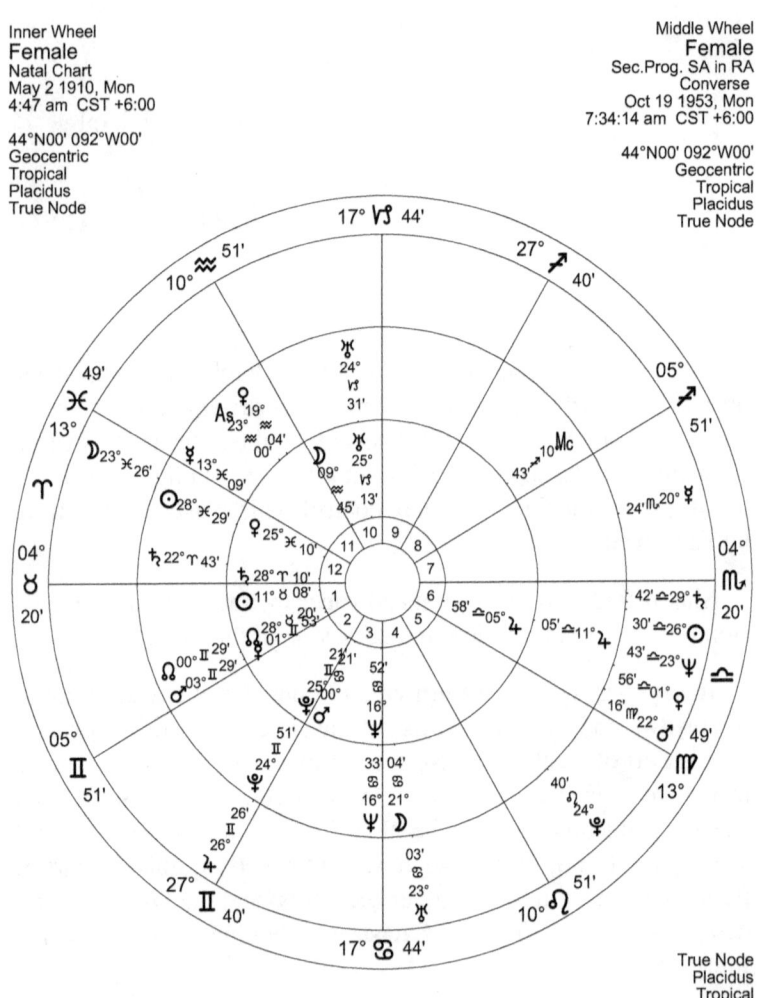

side of the road; opposition Part of Catastrophe and Uranus; square Saturn; part of cardinal T-cross, trine Venus.

Retrograde Jupiter (greater benefic, ruling the eighth of surgery and the ninth of travel) in the sixth house of health, quincunx Ascendant, trine travel Mercury (a saver).

Mars of surgery at critical degree in third house and close to cusp (bringing danger from the left side of the road). (This fits the event so well: the unseen car on the right (Neptune) and the crisis of the out-of-control car from the left (critical Mars). Mars quincunx Fortuna, trine Part of Surgery and Jupiter, semi-sextile Mercury.

Mercury in the first house, dignified in its own sign, trine tenth-house Fortuna (a saver), trine Jupiter and the Moon, air grand trine in air (a saver), rules the sixth house of health, square Part of Surgery (broken arm).

Moon, ruler of fourth house in the tenth, trine Point of Accident, square Sun, semisquare Venus, square Ascendant (abrasions of the eyes).

Point of Greatest Danger in the first (physical) house, conjunct North Node (both at 29 degrees, conjunct the Pleiades and giving something to cry about). There are no planets at the degree of the Nodes.

Fixed Stars
- Uranus conjunct Terrebellum (nature of Venus and Saturn).
- Moon conjunct Bos (nature of Saturn and Venus).
- Mars between Canopus and Wasat (nature of Saturn and Jupiter).

Primary Directions
- Neptune at 29 Leo 44 at same degree as natal lunar Nodes, out-of-rope and square Nodes and Point of Danger.

- Saturn at 11 Gemini 02, semisextile natal Sun.
- Part of Catastrophe at 0 Libra 00, critical degree, square natal Mars.
- Part of Death at 11 Aries 13, semisextile natal Sun.
- Fourth cusp at 29 Leo 51, out-of-rope at same degree as lunar Nodes and square them and Point of Greatest Danger.
- Part of Surgery at critical 42 degrees, semisquare natal Part of Death.

Converse Directions
- Converse Ascendant at 20 Pisces 12, semisextile natal Part of Fatality.
- Converse Sun at 28 Pisces 17, semisextile natal Saturn and natal Part of Death.
- Converse Mars at 17 Taurus 32, trine natal MC and Part of Catastrophe.
- Converse Jupiter at 23 Leo 07, semisextile natal Sun.
- Converse Neptune and fourth cusp at 4 Gemini 02, critical degree.
- Converse Part of Peril at 17 Leo 58, semisextile natal fourth cusp, quincunx Part of Catastrophe and Midheaven.

Tertiary Directions
- Tertiary Ascendant opposition natal Ascendant from natal seventh house, semisextile natal Jupiter, square natal Moon, opposition natal Sun.
- Tertiary Sun conjunct natal eighth cusp, semisextile tertiary Ascendant (a saver), sextile natal Jupiter (a saver), quincunx natal Ascendant.
- Tertiary Uranus, ruler of tertiary fourth, in tertiary third conjunct tertiary Fortuna at the midpoint of tertiary Mercury-Moon, opposition retrograde Neptune in the tertiary ninth house, square natal Saturn, sextile tertiary Jupiter, quincunx tertiary retrograde Pluto, in tertiary eighth.

- Tertiary Mercury, ruler of the tertiary eighth house, opposition natal and tertiary Pluto, sextile tertiary Moon (in the tertiary fourth house conjunct natal Part of Death and square natal Point of Greatest Danger), trine tertiary Pluto, at degree of tertiary Nodes and tertiary Fortuna.
- Tertiary Neptune quincunx tertiary Mercury, quincunx tertiary Moon, forming yod of destiny.
- Tertiary retrograde Mars conjunct tertiary eighth cusp and natal Mercury; square natal Part of Surgery; opposition tertiary Sun; trine natal Jupiter, Moon, and Fortuna; semisextile natal Mars.
- Tertiary Venus trine tertiary Moon and natal and tertiary Pluto, forming grand trine in air and backing up the natal air grand trine (a saver).
- Tertiary retrograde Saturn conjunct natal Sun, trine natal and tertiary Uranus, opposition tertiary Jupiter, semisextile tertiary Part of Fatality, sextile natal Neptune.

Preceding Eclipses
- January 29, 1953, total lunar eclipse at 9 Leo 48 in radix fourth house opposition natal Moon.
- February 14, 1953, partial solar eclipse at 25 Aquarius 05 in progressed ninth house, trine natal and progressed Pluto, conjunct progressed Uranus.
- July 11, 1953, partial solar eclipse at 18 Capricorn 30 in natal ninth house, conjunct natal MC and Part of Catastrophe, opposition natal and progressed Neptune.
- July 26, 1953, total lunar eclipse at 3 Aquarius 12, conjunct natal Fortuna and Moon, trine natal and progressed Mercury and natal and progressed Jupiter (thus falling into her air grand trine—a saver), square progressed Saturn.
- August 9, 1953, partial solar eclipse at 16 Leo 45 semisextile natal and progressed Neptune, sextile progressed Ascendant.

Secondary Progressions
- Progressed Ascendant-Descendant at critical degree.
- Progressed Venus quincunx Point of Accident.
- Progressed MC-IC at out-of-rope 29 degrees, same degree as natal lunar Nodes, square Nodes and Point of Greatest Danger.
- Progressed Mars at same degree as progressed lunar Nodes.
- Progressed Mercury conjunct natal Mercury, setting off what it promises in the natal chart and activating her air grand trine (a saver).
- Progressed sixth and ninth cusps (hospitals and health) at critical degree.
- Progressed Moon at 13 Virgo 12 semisextile progressed Part of Peril, just past trine to progressed Venus.
- Progressed Sun and natal Sun are not involved, and since the Sun represents life, this helped her to survive the event.

Transits
- Transiting Sun, besieged by transiting Neptune and Saturn, in natal sixth house of health, with Saturn at the degree of the natal lunar Nodes, all three opposition natal Ascendant; square natal, progressed, and tertiary Uranus; opposition natal Saturn; trine natal, progressed, and tertiary Pluto; trine tertiary Moon; quincunx Point of Greatest Danger; square tertiary Neptune.
- Transiting Mercury at the cursed degree trine natal Venus and natal and progressed Neptune; quincunx natal, progressed and tertiary Pluto; opposition tertiary Saturn; quincunx progressed Ascendant; semisextile tertiary enus.
- Transiting lunar Nodes at same degree as natal Saturn, tertiary lunar Nodes, and tertiary Moon and Pluto.
- Transiting Jupiter conjunct natal, progressed, and tertiary Pluto in tertiary eighth house; quincunx tertiary Jupiter; sextile natal Saturn and progressed Mars; quincunx natal, progressed, and teritiary Uranus; square natal Venus;

semisquare natal Sun and progressed Venus.
- Transiting Uranus opposition natal, progressed, and tertiary Uranus; conjunct progressed Mars; trine natal Venus; square natal Saturn; conjunct tertiary Neptune; quincunx tertiary Mercury.
- Transiting Pluto trine tertiary Mercury; opposition tertiary Moon; square tertiary Jupiter; trine natal Saturn; quincunx natal, progressed, and tertiary Uranus.
- Transiting Mars opposition natal Venus, quincunx progressed Part of Catastrophe, square progressed Ascendant and tertiary Mercury.
- Transiting Venus trine natal and progressed Mercury and tertiary Mars, quincunx natal Ascendant, conjunct natal and progressed Jupiter, trine natal Fortuna (a saver).
- Transiting Moon conjunct natal Venus; trine tertiary Neptune; square tertiary Mercury and Part of Catastrophe, and natal, progressed, and tertiary Pluto; sextile natal, progressed, and tertiary Uranus.

Chapter 23

Car Accident

On April 13, 1972, at approximately 3:00 pm, Nancy was driving through an intersection when another car, making a left turn, struck her rear fender. Nancy suffered a bruised chest, and her spleen was mangled. A piece of her tongue was bitten off, and she had a deep cut on her right index finger which became infected and then gangrenous. The gangrene was finally arrested, and she was on the critical list for 15 days.

In the chart we find the Ascendant, Mercury, and the Sun in violent Aries, while the Point of Accident and Part of Peril Pluto are in violent Capricorn, and the Point of Greatest Danger falls in the seventh house of other people, in violent Scorpio.

Venus, the lesser benefic, also rises in the map, strong in its own sign (a saver). It is quincunx retrograde Jupiter (blood) in the sixth of health, the latter being disposited by Venus, which is also square retrograde Neptune.

Pluto at the same degree as the lunar Nodes straddles the cusp of the fourth house (also at the degree of the nodes). It rules the eighth of surgery with Mars as its co-ruler, giving two Parts of Peril. It is sextile Venus, square the Saturn-Jupiter conjunction, both retrograde in the sixth house, and also square the rising Sun and Mercury, being the fulcrum of a cardinal cross by a translation of light.

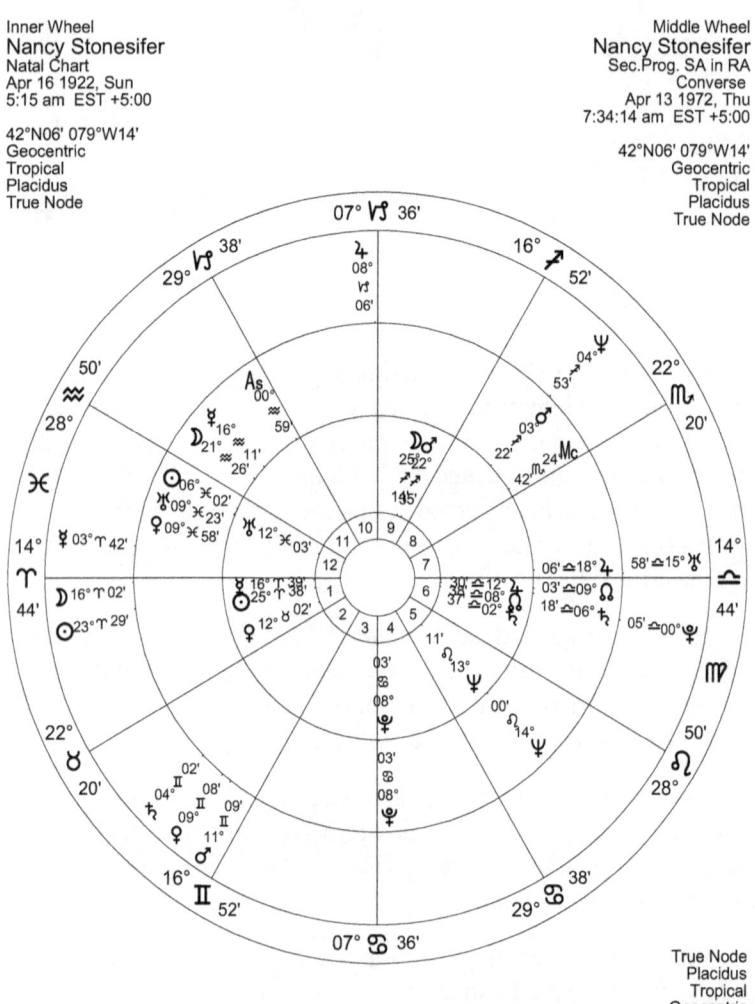

Mars, ruler of the Ascendant, is trine the Sun and conjunct the Moon in the transportation sign of Sagittarius in the ninth (travel) house. The third and ninth cusps are at a critical degree.

The Sun and Moon are in an exact trine, and both of them, along with Mars and Mercury, are trine retrograde Neptune, forming a fire grand trine (a saver).

The sixth and twelfth cusps are at the out-of-rope 29 degrees, while Uranus, ruling and in the twelfth, is conjunct the Parts of Catastrophe and Death, opposition the Part of Fatality, quincunx the sixth-house Jupiter, and sextile Venus, thus forming a yod (destiny aspect). Uranus is also trine the Point of Greatest Danger and widely square the ninth-house Mars.

The Point of Greatest Danger is at a critical degree, conjunct Part of Peril Pluto.

Fixed Stars
- Sun conjunct Alpherg (nature of Saturn and Jupiter).
- Neptune conjunct Acubens (nature of Saturn and Mercury).
- Mars between two stars: Rasal Hague (nature of Saturn and Mars, and Lesath (nature of Mercury and Mars).
- Moon conjunct Aculeus (nature of Mars and Moon).

Primary Directions
- Ascendant at 4 Gemini 13, critical degree.
- Mercury at 5 Gemini 57, opposition natal Fortuna, semisextile Part of Peril Mars, sesquisquare Point of Accident.
- Pluto at 27 Leo 20, semisquare natal Saturn.
- Neptune at 2 Libra 29, conjunct natal Saturn.
- Mars at 11 Aquarius 07, trine natal Jupiter.
- Part of Peril Pluto at 10 Pisces 09, semisquare natal Sun.
- Part of Death at 2 Taurus 23, quincunx natal Saturn.

Converse Directions
- Converse Ascendant at 26 Aquarius 09, semisextile Point of Greatest Danger.
- Converse Mercury at 27 Aquarius 23, sesquisquare natal Jupiter.
- Converse Venus at 22 Pisces 47, square natal Mars.
- Converse Saturn at 13 Leo 20, conjunct natal Neptune.
- Converse Jupiter at 23 Leo 12, semisquare natal Pluto.
- Converse Moon at 5 Scorpio 57, trine natal Part of Peril Mars, semisextile natal Fortuna.
- Converse Part of Peril Mars at 26 Taurus 08, trine Point of Greatest Danger.

Tertiary Directions
- Tertiary Ascendant in natal tenth house, square natal Mercury, quincunx tertiary Neptune, sextile tertiary Uranus.
- Tertiary Mercury rises in the tertiary chart, conjunct natal Point of Greatest Danger and part of Surgery. It rules tertiary eighth house and the critical tertiary fifth and eleventh houses, square natal Sun, semisextile natal Moon.
- Tertiary Sun rising in tertiary first, intercepted and sextile natal Mars, Moon and Sun (at the midpoint of natal Sun and Moon); square natal eighth cusp, opposition Neptune.
- Tertiary Moon in tertiary fourth house, ruler of tertiary seventh of open enemies, square tertiary Sun and Neptune; fulcrum of a fixed T-cross in the tertiary chart.
- Tertiary Pluto opposition tertiary Ascendant from tertiary sixth house, trine natal and tertiary Uranus, quincunx conjunction of tertiary Mars and Jupiter.
- Tertiary Mars and Jupiter in natal eighth house, trine natal Mercury and tertiary Neptune, square tertiary Uranus, quincunx tertiary Moon.
- Tertiary stationary retrograde Saturn at same degree as tertiary lunar Nodes, in natal eighth house and tertiary ninth, semisquare tertiary Mars and Jupiter, widely opposition

tertiary Moon, semisextile natal Saturn, square tertiary Part of Catastrophe.
- Tertiary Venus exalted but at out-of-rope 29 degrees and void of course.
- Tertiary Part of Catastrophe at critical degree, quincunx natal and progressed Pluto, trine natal Jupiter, opposition natal Neptune.
- Tertiary Part of Peril and Fortuna conjunction conjunct tertiary third cusp, trine natal and tertiary Neptune, opposition natal Jupiter, quincunx progressed Point of Greatest Danger, square natal and tertiary Pluto.
- Tertiary Part of Fatality opposition tertiary Venus, sextile natal Point of Accident.

Preceding Eclipses
- July 6, 1971, total lunar eclipse at 13 Aquarius 30 trine progressed Sun, progressed Ascendant, and natal Jupiter; opposition natal and progressed Neptune; semisextile natal and progressed Uranus and natal Part of Death.
- July 26, 1971, partial lunar eclipse at 2 Aquarius 00 trine natal Saturn, square progressed Part of Death, sesquisquare critical natal third cusp.
- January 16, 1972, total solar eclipse as 25 Capricorn 25 conjunct Point of Accident, square natal Sun, semisextile natal Moon.
- January 30, 1972, partial lunar eclipse at 9 Leo 00, critical degree, semisextile natal Pluto and fourth cusp.

Secondary Progressions
- Progressed Ascendant conjunct progressed Sun and both square natal Part of Greatest Danger and progressed Uranus, sextile natal and progressed Neptune.
- Progressed Mercury changing signs at critical degree in natal third house, square critical progressed Saturn (turning stationary direct).

- Progressed Jupiter conjunct natal North Node (a saver) by retrograde motion, square natal and progressed Pluto and natal fourth cusp.
- Progressed fourth cusp semisquare progressed Venus.
- Progressed Mars trine Part of Catastrophe.
- Progressed Fortuna at 5 Libra 26 sextile natal Fortuna (a saver).

Transits

- Transiting Sun conjunct natal Sun in natal first house (a saver), in tertiary third house, square tertiary Mercury and natal Point of Accident, trine natal Moon (a saver).
- Transiting Moon (New Moon day) in natal first house conjunct natal Ascendant and Mercury; trine natal Mars, Mercury, and Moon (transiting Sun and Moon setting off the natal grand trine—a saver); trine tertiary Neptune.
- Transiting Saturn at critical degree trine progressed Moon and Fortuna, conjunct critical tertiary fifth cusp, quincunx tertiary Saturn and Venus.
- Transiting Venus semisextile natal, progressed, and tertiary Pluto, natal fourth cusp, and progressed Venus; at same degree as Jupiter; sextile natal and progressed Neptune.
- Transiting Mars (in travel sign Gemini with transiting Saturn and Venus) sextile natal and progressed Neptune; semisextile natal, progressed, and tertiary Pluto and progressed Venus; conjunct progressed Ascendant and Sun from the twelfth house; quincunx tertiary Part of Catastrophe; square progressed Part of Peril Pluto; trine natal Jupiter; sesquisquare Point of Accident and tertiary Mercury; opposition tertiary Mars and Jupiter.
- Transiting retrograde Pluto at critical degree conjunct progressed Saturn, square progressed Mercury, semisextile tertiary Saturn, quincunx progressed Sun.
- Transiting retrograde Uranus conjunct natal seventh cusp, opposition natal Ascendant and Mercury, quincunx natal

and progressed Uranus and tertiary Mars and Jupiter, trine progressed Ascendant and Sun, sextile natal and progressed Neptune.
- Transiting retrograde Neptune at critical degree in natal eighth house, conjunct natal Fortuna, sextile progressed Moon, conjunct critical tertiary eleventh cusp.
- Transiting Jupiter at degree of natal lunar Nodes conjunct natal MC; square natal and progressed Jupiter; opposition natal, progressed, and tertiary Pluto; square natal Ascendant; in the tertiary twelfth house.
- Transiting lunar Nodes at degree of natal Part of Catastrophe.
- Transiting Mercury in natal twelfth house opposition natal and progressed Saturn; square progressed Mercury and natal, progressed, and tertiary Pluto; square natal fourth cusp; quincunx tertiary Saturn.

Summary

In comparing the data of those who survived with those who didn't, we find either a lack of T-square involvement in those who survived or more of the mutable involvment.

In the examples of those who survived their experience, there are three charts with no T-square. Three have cardinal crosses, and only one has a fixed cross. The remainder contain mutable crosses, and one chart even has two of them, while one contains a grand square.

Five charts have grand trines, three of them in the air element and two in fire, all savers, especially if one of the planets ties in to the T-cross, because they are automatically set off at the same time as the crosses. Four charts contain a yod (aspect of destiny), showing a karmic payment.

In both, some charts have two Parts of Peril, signifying double jeopardy or danger from two distinctly different areas.

Thus it seems that although the potential for a so-called accidental event is present in the charts of those who survived, the predominance of mutability gives them the potential to escape or avoid the finality shown in those who didn't survive.

www.ingramcontent.com/pod-product-compliance
Lightning Source LLC
Chambersburg PA
CBHW020759160426
43192CB00006B/385